Understanding Racial and Ethnic Groups

Critical Thinking and Analysis

William Egelman

Iona College

Allyn and Bacon

Boston • London • Toronto • Sydney • Tokyo • Singapore

Series Editor: *Jeff Lasser*
Editorial Assistant: *Andrea Christie*
Marketing Manager: *Jackie Aaron*
Editorial-Production Administrator: *Gordon Laws*
Composition Buyer: *Linda Cox*
Electronic Composition: *Peggy Cabot, Cabot Computer Services*
Manufacturing Buyer: *Suzanne Lareau*
Cover Administrator: *Kristina Mose-Libon*

Library of Congress Cataloging-in-Publication Data

Egelman, William.
    Understanding racial and ethnic groups : critical thinking and analysis /
    William Egelman.
        p.   cm.
    Includes bibliographical references.
    ISBN 0-205-33352-4 (pbk.)
        1. United States—Race relations.   2. United States—Ethnic relations.
    3. Minorities—United States—Social conditions.   4. Minorities—United States—
    History.   I. Title.

    E184.A1 E364 2001
    305.8'00973—dc21   2001022763

Printed in the United States of America

10   9   8   7   6   5   4   3   2   1   05   04   03   02   01   00

Contents

Preface

This book began almost thirty years ago when I first started teaching on the college level. The first advanced Sociology course I ever taught was a course in Race and Ethnic Relations. I have taught it every year since 1972. All the students I have taught in this course are, in a sense, contributors to this work. Their questions, observations, and discussions helped to shape my own thinking in the field.

During the fall, 2000 semester I had a group of 22 students in the course. They served as "guinea pigs" for this work. They went through all of the chapters. They did the exercises, made comments, offered editorial judgments, and helped to set their professor straight on a number of occasions. I would like to acknowledge their contribution to this work by placing their names in print: Shaun Adams, Drew Albaugh, Jennifer Alves, Michelle Alves, Scott Cweklinski, Christine Farrell, Liza Gallardo, Talia Gallardo, Jennifer Habermann, Elisvan Hernandez, Hillari Javor, Nicole Jimenez, Christopher John, Andrew Kelly, Yvette Maldonado, Juanita Perkins, Colette Phipps, Sara Pixley, Gregory Preddie, Hasan Tariq, Christina Torrieri, Jason Tulinski.

In addition, I would like to thank my colleagues at the *Iona College Center for Social Research*, Meryl Nadel, William Gratzer, Brian Nickerson, and Michael D'Angelo for allowing me to use the data derived from the Center's annual survey for inclusion in Chapter 8 of this book.

I would also like to thank the following reviewers for their helpful and insightful comments: William L. Smith, Georgia Southern University; Clifford L. Broman, Michigan State University; Levon Chorbajian, University of Massachusetts—Lowell. The editorial staff at Allyn & Bacon was of enormous help and I was lucky to have their assistance in this project.

Lastly, there are five people I would like to thank. To my parents, now both deceased, I owe an eternal debt of gratitude for the values they instilled in me. In a real sense, everything I do I do as a legacy for my sons, Aaron and Jeremy. I hope they learn by my mistakes and benefit from any right turns I may have made. The ideas expressed in the introduction are directed to all the readers of this book, but especially to my own children. And, to Connie, the understatement of the year, thanks for everything.

Introduction

Unlike most introductions to textbooks, I would like to address the reader by making some personal observations. I began teaching at Iona College almost thirty years ago. The first advanced course in Sociology I ever taught was a course on Race and Ethnic Relations. It is my favorite course, and on a personal note, it is for me the most meaningful course I teach. Let me explain why.

My parents were immigrants. My father came from Poland in 1905 when he was two years old. My mother came from Russia in 1921 at the age of 14. Their families came here, as did other immigrants, to achieve a better life. In their case, the major motivation was to escape religious persecution. When I was growing up, I can vividly recall stories my mother told me about having to hide in a gentile neighbor's cellar to avoid being killed. From time to time the Jews who lived in the area were subjected to pogroms or organized attacks. If they were found, they would have been subjected to substantial physical abuse and even death. Therefore, my ancestors came to America seeking religious freedom.

I spent the first part of my childhood living in an area of New York City called the South Bronx. This was immediately after World War II. The German attempt to destroy all Jewish life in Europe, called the Holocaust, was a topic of almost daily conversation in my home. This attempt to destroy Jews and others—Poles, Russians, Gypsies, Gays—was not an abstract historical event. It was very real and very personal, and even as a child, I felt it deeply.

In the mid-1950s another series of events made a lasting impact on me. This was what was then called the Negro Civil Rights Movement. This was the attempt by African Americans, helped in part by other Americans, to achieve equality. On our little black and white television set each night I would watch black men and women being stopped at courthouse steps because they wanted to register to vote. I would see black men, women and even children shoved and beaten because they wanted to sit at certain seats in a restaurant. I saw young children and college age students barred from entering schools because of the color of their skin.

In the mind of a young child, me, the events of the Holocaust and the treatment of African Americans merged. I saw them as part of a larger problem, the problem of intolerance. Therefore finding myself some forty years later teaching courses in Race and Ethnic Relations and doing much of my research and writing in this area is perhaps not all that surprising.

These early experiences have certainly influenced my worldview. We live in a pluralistic world made up of a variety of ethnic, immigrant, and racial groups. In all likelihood your fellow students are an example of a cross section of these populations. Some people become very disturbed at such diversity. They feel threatened by those who are different. They become ethnocentric in their outlook, and anyone who is not like them is perceived to be inferior. These people desire homogeneity and sameness.

In practical demographic terms, these people are very unrealistic. Approximately one out of five human beings is Chinese. Approximately two out of five human beings are either Chinese or Asian Indian. Even in the United States, there is growing diversity in the population. Terms like black, white, and Hispanic mask a much greater diversity. Within the category black, there are the descendents of the enslaved peoples of Africa, the dark-skinned immigrants from the Caribbean and Latin America, and the small but growing numbers of immigrants from a variety of African nations. In the white category, there are Italian Americans, Jewish Americans, Irish Americans, and a wide variety of other ethnic-immigrant groups. The Hispanic category, too, is made up of a variety of distinct groups including, among others, Cuban Americans, Puerto Rican Americans, and Mexican Americans.

I must confess to you that I find this type of variety stimulating. Sameness, I find, is quite boring. Even aesthetically, I like to see people who look different from one another. I enjoy a technicolor world and the cultural cafeteria of places like New York City and other major cities. Such diversity, I believe enriches a culture, and ultimately all the people who live in the culture.

Why do so many people fear this type of diversity? In a nutshell I believe the answer lies in the following: ignorance breeds a kind of paranoia, which leads to the development of prejudice that eventuates in discrimination. As college students and hopefully as college graduates, it is important for you to become aware of this process, and as educated adults you should be capable of accomplishing the following:

> *When you see ignorance, inform it*
> *When you see paranoia, treat it*
> *When you see prejudice, confront it*
> *When you see discrimination, condemn it*

One may look upon these suggested actions as constituting a lifelong assignment. Ultimately, prejudice and intolerance should be seen as an insult to us all. Among an educated populace schooled in democratic ideals such behavior should never be condoned.

This book will allow the reader to explore a variety of issues related to Race and Ethnic Relations. It will give you the opportunity to examine both historical and contemporary data, and to review the experiences of a number of groups, both racial and ethnic, which are part of the diverse population of the United States. If the goal of creating a more tolerant society is to be achieved, it must be based on a foundation of knowledge. Hopefully, this book will contribute to that end.

I would like to add an additional bibliographic note. The introductions to each chapter are based on some twenty-eight years of teaching courses on Race and Ethnic Relations. The information is derived from a variety of sources and my own research and interpretations. At the end of each chapter I include a "Selected Bibliography and Suggested Readings" section for those students wishing to further investigate some of the issues raised in these chapters. The data sources for the analysis sections are presented in footnotes in the tables.

1

The Development of Slavery

Slavery is an ancient phenomenon. Ancient Hebrew society, Greece, Rome, and much of the Islamic world had systems of slavery. The Old Testament even goes so far as to outline the rights and privileges of slaves. In many societies, the persons who were enslaved were seen as property, and at the same time, they still maintained their sense of humanity. As in ancient Hebrew society, slaves were seen as people, and they had certain rights. They were not to be abused, and to some degree the laws of the society protected their physical well-being.

This is not to suggest that slavery was a status to which one would want to aspire. For most of history slaves could be bought, sold, traded, leased, and even inherited. Slavery was part of everyday life. It was a norm, and in many societies it was part of the historical tradition. The system of slavery that emerged in the British colonies of North America was, in part, a continuation of a long historical system, and at the same time, something quite different. In many ways this new system of slavery was much more rigid than the systems that came before it.

How did such a system emerge? In the late Middle Ages Europeans began to look beyond their own continent, and they began to explore other lands. Largely motivated by the desire for economic gain they began to seek out new trading routes with the East. The Portuguese initially led this effort. Soon, the Spanish joined in the exploration of new trade routes to the East. Seeking this new trade route to the East, Portuguese sailors sailed along the west coast of Africa, around the southern tip of the continent, and into the Indian Ocean. Along the way these Portuguese sailors began trading in goods with the local inhabitants. In stops all along the West African coast they would trade in a variety of items. The slave trade became a part of this trade activity. Given the economic structure of Western Europe, there was not a great demand for slaves. Europe was emerging out of feudalism and the preconditions for what would become the Industrial Revolution were developing. Therefore, the need for slaves was not great. In fact between the 1400s and 1600s the demand for slaves in Western Europe declined.

The enslavement of African peoples might very well have ceased at that point. Then, Columbus sailed the ocean blue, and Europe discovered the "New

World." This New World, with its very warm climate and rich soil had great potential for agricultural development. The crop that initially spurred on the desire for slaves was sugar. Europe had developed a sweet tooth, and the demand for the crop was very high. Therefore, there was the potential for great profits to be made. However, sugar cane cultivation is labor intensive, and large numbers of laborers are needed to make sugar cane production profitable. The African slaves encountered on the west coast of Africa were just the human resource the Portuguese and Spanish needed to work the oppressive sugar cane plantations of the Caribbean region and Brazil.

Thus began the famous or infamous triangle trade. African slaves would be sent to the Caribbean for sugar. The sugar would be shipped to Europe in exchange for manufactured goods. These manufactured goods would be shipped to Africa in exchange for slaves. Substantial profits could be made at each point where business transactions occurred.

The British came rather late to the slave trade. Eventually they took control of many of the islands in the Caribbean, and along with the Dutch, they continued the profitable trade in sugar. Tobacco, as well as other crops, now became part of the agricultural system of the islands. In the early 1600s the British began to settle the east coast of North America. The climate and land, especially of the southern colonies, were similar to that of the islands. Tobacco, rice, indigo, and other crops were grown. As with sugar, Europe had also developed a strong desire for tobacco. Again, this type of agricultural activity was labor intensive, and the British saw the usefulness of using African slaves for this system.

How could the enslaving of a people be justified? Why were Africans selected for this dubious distinction? There is no consensus among scholars as to why this happened. Certain factors, however, appear to have been critical in the development of the African slave trade in the American colonies.

First, Africans were different. Their physical attributes were markedly different from the British. This was a unique aspect of this new slave system. West Africans are among the most dark-skinned peoples of the world. Their facial features, skin tone, type and amount of body hair were not like those of the British. In ancient systems of slavery very often masters and slaves were very similar in physical appearance. Societies went to war with their neighbors, and dramatic physical distinctions may not have been readily apparent. In many ancient cultures slaves had to wear special clothing to set them apart from the non-slave groups. This was necessary because there were no distinctive features of the slave classes. With the importation of Africans as slaves, this was no longer an issue. Their physical differences further legitimated their slave status.

In addition, the darkness of their skin tone heightened negative perceptions. In the English language and in the mind of the English people blackness is associated with dirt, filth, danger, and other negative concepts. For many of the British settlers, black skin represented a whole repertoire of undesirable characteristics.

A second factor that contributed to the enslavement of Africans was their cultural differences. The British viewed the Africans as heathens. They were seen as unbelievers. They were non-Christian. This heathenism was equated with savagery or barbaric behavior. They were seen as "uncivilized."

A third factor leading to the development of this slave system was economic motivation. Europe had a great desire for the products produced in the New World. Sugar and tobacco were in great demand throughout much of Europe. The profit motive drove the slave system. There were enormous fortunes to be made. In addition, the plantation system that emerged was a labor-intensive system. Therefore, for profits to be made, there was a need for large numbers of workers. The slave system provided relatively low-cost labor that would contribute to greater profits. Given the perception of Africans, they were particularly vulnerable to being subjected to this system.

Ironically, within the British system of jurisprudence there was no legal position called slave. In a sense, slavery had to be invented in the colonies. The process by which slavery became a legal institution in the British colonies has not been clearly delineated. In the early 1600s it is unclear whether or not slaves were in the colonies. Certainly during the early stages of settlement there was no formal institution of slavery. What is known, is that by the end of the seventeenth century, slavery had become a recognized legal institution in the colonies. The slave system was supported by an entire system of laws and court decisions. By 1700 there was no question as to its legitimacy.

This chapter will give readers the opportunity to examine some of the population data of the time period. By examining these data readers may gain some insight into how many people were involved in this process and which colonies were most important in the development of the slave system.

One final word on language usage. The descendents of the enslaved peoples of West Africa are categorized by a variety of terms: African American, Black American, and Afro American, among others. In this chapter the term Negro will be used because it was the term used during the historical period covered in this chapter.

Analysis

TABLE 1.1   *Estimated White and Negro Population of American Colonies: 1630–1700; 1780*

Year	White	Negro
1630	4,586	60
1640	26,037	597
1660	72,138	2,920
1680	144,536	6,971
1700	223,071	27,817
1780	2,204,949	575,420

Source: U.S. Bureau of the Census. *Historical Statistics of the United States.* Washington, D.C., 1975.

1. Table 1.1 presents data on population estimates for the American colonies during the seventeenth century, and for 1780. Calculate the percent of the Negro population for each of the years listed in Table 1.1A. Place your answers in Table 1.1A Remember to total the rows and then divide the Negro population by the total population. For example:

$$\text{First (for 1630): } 4{,}586 + 60 = 4{,}646. \text{ Then: } \frac{60}{4{,}646} \times 100 = 1.3 \text{ percent}$$

TABLE 1.1A   *Percent Negro Population in American Colonies: 1630–1700; 1780*

Year	Percent Negro
1630	
1640	
1660	
1680	
1700	
1780	

2. How would you describe the pattern you found in Table 1.1A?

3. What factors do you believe contributed to the growth of the Negro population?

TABLE 1.2   *Estimated Negro Population of Selected American Colonies: 1640–1700; 1780*

	Maryland		Virginia		All Colonies
	Number	Percent	Number	Percent	Number
1640	20		150		597
1660	758		950		2,920
1680	1,611		3,000		6,971
1700	3,227		16,390		27,817
1780	80,515		220,568		575,420

Source: U.S. Bureau of the Census. *Historical Statistics of the United States.* Washington, D.C., 1975.

4. Table 1.2 presents data for Maryland and Virginia, two of the major slave-holding colonies during the seventeenth century. Calculate the percent distribution of Negroes in the colonies of Maryland and Virginia.

5. What percent of all Negroes were in the two colonies combined for all years listed?

1640_____   1660_____   1680_____   1700_____   1780_____

6. Why do you believe these two colonies account for such a large proportion of the entire Negro population?

TABLE 1.3   *Estimated White and Black Populations in American Colonies: 1640–1700; 1780*

	Maryland		Virginia	
	Negro	*White*	*Negro*	*White*
1640	20	563	150	10,292
1660	758	7,666	950	26,070
1680	1,611	16,293	3,000	40,596
1700	3,227	26,377	16,390	42,170
1780	80,515	164,959	220,582	317,422

Source: Bureau of the Census. *Historical Statistics of the United States.* Washington, D.C., 1975.

7. Calculate the ratios of black to white populations for each of the colonies for the years listed in Table 1.3.

Use the following formula:

$$\frac{\text{White Population}}{\text{Negro Population}} = \text{Black/White Ratio}$$

TABLE 1.3A   *Negro and White Ratios for Selected American Colonies: 1640–1700; 1780*

Year	Maryland	Virginia
1640		
1660		
1680		
1700		
1780		

8. Describe the overall trend you find in Table 1.3A.

9. By the early nineteenth century, slavery in the South had been fully institution-alized. However, not all Negroes were slaves. In the northern states slavery no longer existed; while in the southern states some small number of Negroes were given their freedom. Let us take a closer look at the process of manumission. Table 1.4 presents data on the Free Negro and Slave population. Calculate the percent distribution in each category for both males and females and place the results in Table 1.4A.

Remember, you need to add the free and slave categories and then divide each category by the total. For example:

Free Male distribution (for 1820): 112,734 + 788,028 = 900,762

$$\frac{112,734}{900,762} \times 100 = 12.5 \, \text{percent}$$

TABLE 1.4 *Free and Slave Population: 1820–1860*

Year	Males		Females	
	Free	*Slave*	*Free*	*Slave*
1820	112,734	788,028	120,790	750,010
1830	153,453	1,012,823	166,146	996,220
1840	186,481	1,246,517	199,822	1,240,938
1850	208,724	1,602,534	225,771	1,601,779
1860	234,119	1,982,625	253,951	1,971,135

Source: U.S. Bureau of the Census. *Historical Statistics of the United States.* Washington, D.C., 1975.

TABLE 1.4A *Percent Distribution of Free and Slave Population*

	Males		Females	
	Free	Slave	Free	Slave
1820				
1830				
1840				
1850				
1860				

10. What overall pattern do you find in the distribution of the Negro population during the early 1800s?

11. What factors might have lead to the manumission of some of the slaves during the time period covered in the table?

12. What impact did the development of slavery have on American society during the seventeenth and eighteenth centuries?

*Selected Bibliography and Suggested Readings*_____

Blassingame, John W. *The Slave Community: Plantation Life in the Ante-Bellum South*. New York: Oxford University Press, 1972.

Davidson, Basil. *The African Slave Trade*. Boston: Little, Brown & Company, 1980.

Higginbotham, Leon A., Jr. *Shades of Freedom: Racial Politics and Presumptions of the American Legal Process*. New York: Oxford University Press, 1996.

———. *In the Matter of Color: Race and the American Legal Process: The Colonial Period*. New York: Oxford University Press, 1978.

Jordan, Winthrop. *The White Man's Burden: Historical Origins of Racism in the United States*. New York: Oxford University Press, 1974.

Kolchin, Peter. *American Slavery, 1619–1877*. New York: Hill & Wang, 1993.

Rose, Willie Lee, ed. *A Documentary History of Slavery in North America*. New York: Oxford University Press, 1976.

Stampp, Kenneth. *The Peculiar Institution: Slavery in the Ante-Bellum South*. New York: Vintage Books, 1956.

Wood, Betty. *The Origins of American Slavery: Freedom and Bondage in the English Colonies*. New York: Hill & Wang, 1997.

2

Early Immigration Patterns

A Nation of Immigrants

The United States has long been considered "a nation of immigrants." Native Americans emigrated from Asia thousands of years ago. In the sixteenth century Spanish and French explorers, along with small numbers of settlers, arrived. In the early seventeenth century, the English began to settle on the east coast of North America. While they were one of a number of different groups, the English quickly became the dominant group in the colonies. Peoples from Africa also came to the colonies but they were part of the forced migration stream that was to make up the slave population of the southern colonies. By and large it was the English who were to become the model for the new American. American society would emerge as an Anglo American society. To be American was to be English American.

Since those early days of settlement, one might view the history of the United States as a history of immigration. Wave upon wave of immigrants came to these shores. As the data in the analysis section will indicate, there has never been a time when immigrants have not arrived. What does differ is who the immigrants are. Clearly, different groups have arrived at different times.

One of the dominant symbols in American society is the Statue of Liberty, with its arms outstretched, welcoming all newcomers. The reality, however, is a bit more complex. With each immigrant group has come discussion and debate. These debates over immigration appear to focus on three themes. The first theme focuses on economic issues. Some observers believed that new immigrants would take the jobs away from native Americans, in this case not Native Americans in the current sense of the term, but Americans of European ancestry who were already living in the country and who were descended from earlier immigrants. Others believed that immigrants would help stimulate the economy by offering their labor at relatively low cost, and at the same time, increasing the consumer pool for products. By increasing the demand for products, immigrants would help create jobs rather than negatively impacting the job market.

A second theme is related to the culture of society. Nativists, individuals and groups who are opposed to immigration, believed that new immigrants would bring with them their own distinctive cultural traits. They might carry with them behavioral patterns, values, beliefs, and norms that differed from the American value system. Their presence in American society would alter the culture of the society and turn it into something different and alien. The America the nativists loved would no longer exist.

A subsidiary of the cultural theme had to do with the notion of biology and genetics. Many people felt that the pioneer spirit of the earlier immigrants helped to forge a new type of person. This new type of person was genetically superior. This person, called *American*, was the product of all the best that northern and western Europe had to offer and then was forged into a new being by the harsh environment of the settlement experience. Newer immigrants whose area of origin was not the same as the old immigrants were seen as genetically inferior. In a classic racist manner, this view held that no matter what changes were implemented, the natural inferiority of these newcomers could not be overcome. An added element in this argument was the fact that many of the older immigrants were Protestant. A number of the newer immigrants were Catholic, Eastern Orthodox, or Jewish. Religious differences interacted with ethnic differences to further fuel the anti-immigration position.

A third theme that sometimes emerged in these discussions concerned itself with political issues. In this case, there was concern voiced over the possible political domination of the newcomers over the natives. For example, in the anti-immigration literature of the nineteenth century one subject often addressed was the potential political takeover of the country by the Irish Catholics. Some nativists believed that if Catholic immigration were to continue, then eventually the Pope in Rome would rule the United States.

Other factors influenced the perception of new immigrants to the United States. Large numbers of immigrants entering the country in a relatively short time period tended to enhance the anti-immigration furor. If immigrants clustered together in the same settlements they would appear to be larger in number than in fact they were. Critics would argue that they would never be able to assimilate because they stuck together. What is ironic about this argument is that because of prejudice and discriminatory practices, very often immigrants had no choice but to settle in certain restricted areas we now refer to as *ghettoes*.

The degree of difference between the immigrants and the natives also played a role in how the newcomers were perceived. If the immigrants were viewed as being somewhat similar to the natives, they were more highly regarded than those arrivals who were markedly different. As noted above, the English-based model became the model for all Americans. Those immigrants who brought with them cultural attributes that were similar to English American culture were more warmly received than those who did not. Generally speaking, immigrants from Scandinavia—Sweden, Norway, and Denmark—were seen as better candidates for Americanization than those immigrants from places like Poland, Italy, or Greece.

Therefore, a number of factors influenced the immigrant experience. The exercises in this chapter will give the reader the opportunity to chart the different flow of immigrants from the first census in 1790 to the early part of the twentieth century.

Analysis

1. Table 2.1 presents data on the ethnic distribution of the population after the first census was taken in 1790. Calculate the percent of persons who are in each ethnic category.

TABLE 2.1 *Population Distribution by Ethnic Category: 1790*

Ethnic Category	Number	Percent
Total	4,428,220	100.0
English	2,392,891	
Scotch	326,124	
Irish	381,133	
German	341,841	
Dutch	133,593	
French	66,796	
Swedish	27,504	
Negro	758,338	

Source: U.S. Bureau of the Census. *Historical Statistics of the United States.* Washington, D.C., 1975.

2. Which group constitutes the largest category? _____

3. What percent of the population came from the British Isles? _____

4. Why do people from the British Isles constitute the largest group?

5. Table 2.2 presents data on immigration by specific countries or areas of origin. In order to get a sense of patterns of change, place in rank order from highest to lowest, the country with the highest number of immigrants, followed by the country with the second-highest number of immigrants, and so on, for each year shown. Place your answers in Table 2.2A.

TABLE 2.2 *Immigrants by Selected Countries: 1820–1880*

Area of Origin	1820	1840	1860	1880
Great Britain	2,410	2,613	29,737	73,273
Ireland	3,614	39,430	48,637	71,603
Scandinavia	23	207	840	65,657
Germany	968	29,704	54,491	84,638
All others	1,320	12,069	18,765	142,506
Total	8,385	84,066	153,640	457,257

Source: U.S. Bureau of the Census. *Historical Statistics of the United States.* Washington D.C., 1975.

TABLE 2.2A *Rank Order of Immigrants by Area of Origin: 1820–1880*

1820	1840	1860	1880

6. How would you describe the overall pattern of immigration during the period 1820 to 1880?

During the early years of the twentieth century the United States experienced a substantial increase in the number of immigrants arriving to these shores. There were four years when over 1,100,000 immigrants arrived. Let us next examine and analyze these peak years of immigration.

TABLE 2.3   *Immigration During Peak Years by Area of Origin: Early 1900s*

Area of Origin	1906	1907	1913	1914
Great Britain	67,198	79,037	60,328	48,729
Ireland	34,995	34,530	27,876	24,688
Scandinavia	52,781	52,781	32,267	29,391
Germany	37,564	37,564	34,329	35,734
Poland[1]	265,138	338,452	254,825	278,152
Eastern Europe (including Russia)	215,665	258,943	291,040	255,660
Italy	273,120	285,731	265,542	283,738
All others	154,274	193,311	231,685	262,388
Total	1,100,735	1,285,349	1,197,892	1,218,480

[1]Between 1899 and 1919, data on Poland includes Austria-Hungary, Germany, and Russia. Also includes data from other Central European countries. This is due to the political domination of Poland by other European societies.

Source: U.S. Bureau of the Census. *Historical Statistics of the United States.* Washington, D.C., 1975.

7. For the years shown, what percent of all immigrants arrived from Poland?

    1906_____   1907_____   1913_____   1914_____

8. What percent came from Eastern Europe including Russia?

    1906_____   1907_____   1913_____   1914_____

9. What percent came from Italy?

    1906_____   1907_____   1913_____   1914_____

10. Now place all the countries shown in rank order as you did in Table 2.2A.

TABLE 2.3A *Rank Order of Immigrants for Selected Years*

1906	1907	1913	1914

11. Which countries were the major areas of origin for immigrants during the peak years shown in Tables 2.3 and 2.3A?

12. Why do you believe these countries became the major areas of origin for immigrants to the United States?

13. Compare the information in Table 2.2 with the information in Table 2.3. Which groups were dominant in the earlier period of immigration as compared to the more recent period?

Selected Bibliography and Suggested Readings

Costello, Lawrence and Stanley Feldstein, eds. *The Ordeal of Assimilation: A Documentary History of the White Working Class, 1830s to the 1970s.* New York: Anchor Press, 1974.

Daniels, Roger. *Coming to America: A History of Immigration and Ethnicity in American Life.* New York: Harper Perennial, 1990.

Dinnerstein, Leonard and David Reimers. *Ethnic Americans: A History of Immigration,* 4th ed. New York: Columbia University Press, 1999.

Gribben, Arthur. *The Great Famine and the Irish Diaspora in America.* Amherst: University of Massachusetts Press, 1999.

Higham, John. *Strangers in the Land: Patterns of American Nativism, 1860–1925.* New Brunswick: Rutgers University Press, 1988.

Irving, Katrina. *Immigrant Mothers: Narratives of Race and Maternity, 1890–1920.* Urbana: University of Illinois Press, 1998.

Jones, Maldwyn. *American Immigration,* 2nd ed. Chicago: University of Chicago Press, 1992.

Takaki, Ronald. *A Different Mirror: A History of Multicultural America.* Boston: Little, Brown, 1993.

Van Vught, William. *Britain to America: Mid-Nineteenth Century Immigration to the United States.* Urbana: University of Illinois Press, 1999.

3

Contemporary
Immigration Patterns
Economic and Cultural Issues

Immigration is one of the most debated issues in today's society. Rarely does a day go by when an elected official or some concerned group does not make pronouncements about the subject of immigration. As with debates that occurred in the last century, there are some groups who favor an open immigration policy, and there are those groups who are opposed to current immigration levels.

Today's debate is remarkably similar to earlier debates. A number of the same issues that were discussed over one hundred years ago are being discussed today. As discussed in the chapter "Early Immigration Patterns," the central themes of this debate appear to focus on economic and cultural issues. Economic issues focus on the availability of work for the newcomers. One question often asked is: are they taking jobs away from Americans? This is a very complex issue. Evidence appears to indicate that immigrants create more work than they take. There is some evidence that Black Americans may lose jobs to the newcomers. However, the research here is far from conclusive.

There is also concern that new immigrants make greater use of public services than they make up for by their tax contributions. For example, their children attend public schools that cost taxpayers money. The taxes the immigrants pay do not pay for the school expenses of their children. The analysis needed to look at this issue is often filled with a number of assumptions, and the assumptions one uses will influence the results one gets. Again, the research evidence here is mixed. A further complication in this issue is related to the distribution of immigrants. If small numbers of immigrants settle in a particular community, the economic impact will, in all likelihood, be negligible. However, if large numbers of immigrants settle in a large city such as Los Angeles or New York City, the economic impact may be sizeable. In addition, sometimes the federal government

will mandate that certain programs be available to citizens and immigrants; however, local governments have to fund these programs. As a result, some local mu-
nicipalities may experience financial pressure.

However, some suggest that even in large cities the cost related to the immigrant population is overstated. Let us use a simple education example to illustrate
the problem. Let us say that a school district has one hundred students. The current school budget is one hundred thousand dollars, or it costs one thousand dollars to educate each student. Ten students, the children of immigrants, enter the
school system. Hypothetically the school budget will now have to increase by ten
thousand dollars to match the one thousand dollars per student cost. In the real
world this is probably not the case. The school buildings are already built. Utility
costs will not increase in proportion to the increase in the number of students.
Some additional costs will be incurred, but these will probably not be in proportion to the added number of students. This hypothetical scenario may not apply if
there is a very large influx of immigrants to one area, impacting the infra-
structure of that area. For example, if the influx of immigrants is so large that a
new school building needs to be constructed, then the financial impact can be
sizeable.

The second theme discussed in the previous century that is also being discussed today is related to American culture. Are the new immigrants capable of
assimilating into American culture? One specific issue related to this theme is
language usage. The state of California passed a bill in 1998 that will largely dis-
mantle the bilingual programs in the state. Non-English-speaking persons will
now have one year to be fully immersed in English language programs. The bill
was motivated by a rather widespread fear that immigrants would retain their
native language and never learn English. Research seems to contradict this
widely held belief. Research indicates that the children of immigrants quickly
learn English, and the second generation has English as their first language. It is
not unusual for members of the first generation (the immigrants) to retain the
language of the Old World. This was true one hundred years ago, and it is still
true today. But just as one hundred years ago the children of the immigrants (the
second generation) made English their first or primary language, so it appears
that is true today.

There appears to be a case of history repeating itself. The debates of old are
the same as the debates of today. Immigration is both an old issue and a contemporary issue. This chapter will allow the reader to examine some of the data on
contemporary immigration patterns and be able to make more informed judgments on the issue of immigration.

Analysis

1. Table 3.1 presents data on immigrants from different regions of the world. Calculate the percent distribution of the immigrants and place your answers in the appropriate cells in the table. This involves a simple calculation. Divide each number by the total number of immigrants for the year shown.

TABLE 3.1　*Legal Immigrants Admitted by Region: 1998*

Region	Number	Percent
Africa	40,660	
Asia	219,696	
Europe	90,793	
North America	252,966	
Caribbean	75,521	
Central America	35,679	
Other North America	141,796	
Oceania	3,935	
South America	45,394	
Unknown	7,003	
Total	660,477	

Source: U.S. Immigration and Naturalization Services. *Legal Immigrants, Fiscal Year 1998.* Annual Report. May 1999.

2. Which two regions send the highest number of immigrants to the United States?

3. Why do you believe these regions are the largest areas of origin?

4. How does this pattern of immigration differ from that seen in the Early Immigration chapter (see Chapter 2)?

5. What specific countries do the new immigrants come from? Table 3.2 lists the top ten sending countries for 1998. Calculate the percentage of immigrants that come from each of the countries.

TABLE 3.2   *Immigrants Admitted by Ten Largest Countries of Origin: 1998*

Country	1998	
	Number	*Percent*
Mexico	131,575	
China	36,884	
India	36,482	
Philippines	34,466	
Dominican Republic	20,387	
Vietnam	17,649	
Cuba	17,375	
Jamaica	15,146	
El Salvador	14,590	
Korea	14,268	
All Immigrants	660,477	

Sources: U.S. Immigration and Naturalization Services. *Annual Report, 1996.* Washington, D.C., 1997; *Legal Immigration, Fiscal Year 1998.* Annual Report. May 1999.

6. Why is Mexico such a predominant source of immigrants?

7. What may be some similarities all ten countries have in common?

TABLE 3.3   *Immigrants Admitted by States of Residence: 1998*

States	Number	Percent
California	170,126	
New York	96,559	
Florida	59,965	
Texas	44,428	
New Jersey	35,091	
Illinois	33,163	
All States	660,477	

Source: U.S. Immigration and Naturalization Services. *Legal Immigration, Fiscal Year 1998.* Annual Report. May 1999.

8. We have analyzed where the recent immigrants are coming from; now, let us look at where they are going. Let us see if there is a settlement pattern that emerges after we examine the data in Table 3.3. First, calculate the percent distribution of immigrants to the top six receiving states. Place your answers directly in the table.

9. Why are these six states the major areas of destination for immigrants?

10. Why are California and New York the largest areas of destination?

11. As we have seen California and New York are the major areas of destination for immigrants. However, both states are large, and it may not be the case that immigrants are distributed evenly throughout each state. Let us look at two major metropolitan areas (cities and their surrounding suburbs) to gain further insight into the settlement patterns of immigrants. Examine the data in Table 3.4, and calculate the percent of immigrants that settle in each of the areas.

TABLE 3.4 *Immigrants Admitted by Selected Metropolitan Areas: 1998*

Metropolitan Area	Number	Percent
New York, NY	82,175	
Los Angeles-Long Beach, CA	59,598	
All States	660,477	

Source: U.S. Immigration and Naturalization Services. *Legal Immigration, Fiscal Year 1998.* Annual Report. May 1999.

12. Why do these two metropolitan areas attract such a large proportion of all the immigrants that enter the United States?

TABLE 3.5 *Percent Employed Persons by Occupation, Natives and Immigrants: 1996*

Occupational Category	Natives	Immigrants
Total Employed	126,708,000	314,705
Managerial and Professional Specialty; Technical, Sales, and Administrative Support[1]	58.5	45.1
Service Occupations	13.6	19.3
Precision Production, Craft, and Repair	10.7	7.4
Operators, Fabricators, and Laborers	14.4	24.0
Farming, Forestry, and Fishing	2.8	4.2

[1]These categories were collapsed into one large category in order to compare Census data with data from the Immigration and Naturalization Services.

Sources: U.S. Immigration and Naturalization Services. *Annual Report, 1996.* Washington, D.C., 1997; U.S. Bureau of the Census. *Statistical Abstract of the United States: 1997.* Washington, D.C., 1997.

13. What kinds of persons are immigrating to the United States? One characteristic that is important in our society is occupation. Let us look at the occupations of the immigrants and compare them to the occupations of persons already living in the United States. Table 3.5 compares the occupations of immigrants and natives. Examine the table. Do you see some similarities and some differences? What are they?

14. Why are there more immigrants in the categories of service occupations and operators, fabricators, and laborers?

15. How might these new immigrants impact American society, both economically and culturally?

Selected Bibliography and Suggested Readings

Bean, Frank, and Stephanie Bell-Rose, eds. *Immigration and Opportunity: Race, Ethnicity and Employment in the United States.* Albany: Russell Sage, 1999.

Borjas, George. *Friends or Strangers: The Impact of Immigrants on the U.S. Economy.* New York: Basic Books, 1990.

———. *Heaven's Door.* Princeton: Princeton University Press, 1999.

Clark, William. *The California Cauldron: Immigration and the Fortunes of Local Communities.* Guilford: Guilford Publications, 1999.

Foner, Nancy. *New Immigrants in New York.* New York: Columbia University Press, 1987.

Harris, Nigel. *The New Untouchables: Immigration and the New World Worker.* London: Penguin Books, 1995.

Isbister, John. *The Immigration Debate: Rethinking America.* West Hartford: Kumerian Press, 1996.

Smith, James, and Barry Edmundson, eds. *The Immigration Debate: Studies in Economic, Demographic, and Fiscal Effects of Immigration.* National Academic Press, 1998.

Williamson, Chilton, Jr. *The Immigration Mystique: America's False Conscience.* New York: Basic Books, 1996.

4

The Role of Women in Society

The Case for Minority Group Status

Many books written in the field of Race and Ethnic Relations now either include a chapter on women or include discussions of women as part of a number of chapters. Why separate women out for consideration? A number of scholars share the view that women constitute a minority group in American society.

This perspective of women as minority group may have a number of root causes. Interestingly, one of the major impetuses may have been the Civil Rights movement of the post World War II era. Starting in the late 1940s and perhaps culminating in the mid-1960s, Black Americans aggressively sought equal treatment in American society. They, along with a number of white Americans, used a variety of strategies to change the laws of the land. One major goal was to pressure the government to make discriminatory behavior illegal. Federal and local governments responded by passing a number of laws making discrimination in the workplace and other areas illegal. Included in this legislation were not only discriminatory acts against Black Americans but also acts against women and other categories of persons. Therefore, through the legislative process and sometimes supported by the judicial process, women came to be seen as having a position similar to that of Black Americans; that is, they came to be seen as minority groups. Let us examine this idea more closely.

There are three general characteristics that are usually used to define minority groups. First, minority groups have a set of physical and cultural characteristics that set them apart from other members of society. Second, regardless of the size of a minority group, their members have less power in society as compared to other groups. Third, minority group members are often, but not always, victims of prejudice and discrimination.

Many would argue that women in American society and in all countries of the world hold these characteristics in common. First, they do have physical characteristics that set them apart from men. Both in physical appearances and with respect to hormonal characteristics, women are different. Women give birth, men do not. Women experience menstrual flow every month, men do not. Women may also be the stronger of the two sexes. For example, they have the physiological capacity to sustain a fetus for nine months. Obviously, men do not have the same physiological capacity. Also, at least in the United States, women live on average seven years longer than men.

Second, throughout much of history women have been seen as the "second sex." Most societies have reflected patriarchal norms. Patriarchy means that power resides in the male population. This holds true for both power in the family and power in society, generally. This sense of patriarchy has a direct impact on women. Women's position in society is largely a function of what sociologists call *ascribed status*. Status is one's relative position in society. Sociologists determine one's social position by looking at three variables: wealth, education, and occupation. Ascribed status means that one's rights, privileges, and opportunities are determined at birth. One's sex matters because every society has sets of expectations related to whether one is born male or female. These social, cultural, and psychological expectations related to one's sex sociologists call *gender*. In everyday language, what it means to be masculine or feminine is determined by society, and these expectations may be referred to as gender.

The third factor that determines minority group status is that members of the group are victims of prejudice and discrimination. Prejudice may be defined as a negative attitude toward individuals because they are members of a certain group. Prejudice involves both a way of thinking and a way of feeling about others. Discrimination is treating people in a negative manner because of the group to which they belong. Discrimination involves actual behavior, and therefore, it is easier to observe. It results in fewer life chances in a wide variety of areas. Discrimination impacts one's opportunities in education, work, residential location, and earnings potential.

In a more specific manner, how does this minority group status impact women? In a variety of institutional settings, family, government, religion, education, and the economy, women appear to have experienced at least some degree of discrimination. With respect to family, this introduction has already presented a discussion of patriarchy. As one quick example of patriarchal traditions one may cite the fact that when many women marry they take on the last name of their husband. This taking on the husband's name may be connected to the fact that in many cultures of the past wives were the "property" of the husband. In some symbolic way, the name change may be viewed as a kind of cultural branding.

Discriminatory behavior in the political realm may be easily illustrated by the fact that women did not gain the right to vote in the United States until the 1920s. There are a greater number of women holding elected office today than in the past, but all of the major political organs of the Federal, State, and local governmental systems still have clear male majorities even though females are in the majority in the general population.

Males, traditionally, have dominated religious institutions. Women are not permitted to hold higher-status positions in a number of religions. For example, in Roman Catholicism, women cannot become priests, and in Orthodox Judaism, women cannot become rabbis.

Historically, in education women have not been given the same opportunities as men. Higher education has long been seen as a male domain. Even in the 1950s there were relatively few women in colleges and universities in the United States. It was not until the early 1960s that the United States began to see an educational revolution of sorts that included large numbers of women attending institutions of higher learning.

Much has been written about gender inequality in the workplace. Terms like "glass ceiling" and "equal pay for equal work" are now somewhat commonplace. Women, traditionally, have been relegated to lower-status and lower-paying jobs. For example, women became bookkeepers while men became accountants. Women became nurses; men became doctors.

Gender thus appears to have played some role in all of these institutional settings. Put more simply and directly, being female mattered. It put women at some disadvantage compared to their male counterparts. Because gender plays such a decisive role in one's life, sociologists would call gender a *master status*. While we occupy many statuses in life—daughter, lawyer, friend—certain statuses take on much greater meaning with respect to how others identify us and even how we may come to see ourselves. In addition to gender, race and ethnic origin may have also been seen as master statuses. Being male or female, being black or white or Hispanic means something in our society. In many ways it determines how others view you; what life's opportunities may lie before you; and even how you may come to see yourself in the larger sociocultural community.

This chapter will give you the chance to examine how the intersection of gender, race, and ethnic origin may affect the level of achievement in a variety of social settings. Specifically, data on sex, race, and Hispanic origin will be presented along with data on education and income.

Analysis

1. Table 1 presents data on educational attainment by racial/ethnic category and by sex. Calculate the percent distribution of those individuals who have completed a bachelor's degree or more for each ethnic category.

TABLE 4.1 *Educational Attainment of Persons 25 Years Old and Over by Sex, Race, and Hispanic Origin: March 1998*

Ethnic Category	Male			Female		
	Total	College Grad. or More	Percent	Total	College Grad. or More	Percent
White	70,062	19,112		75,016	17,093	
Black	8,578	1,196		10,798	1,662	
Hispanic Origin	8,055	895		7,989	872	

Source: U.S. Census Bureau. *Educational Attainment in the United States.* [online: web], updated March 1998, cited 24 April 2000, pp. 20–513. URL: http://www.census.gov/prod/3/98pubs/p20-513u.pdf

2. Which group has the highest percentage of college graduates or more?

_____

3. Which group has the second highest percent of college graduates or more?

_____

4. Based on the overall findings from Table 4.1, how would you describe the relationships between ethnic category, sex, and educational attainment?

5. Educational attainment is related to income. Generally the higher one's education, the higher one's earnings will be. Does this hold true equally for men and women? Examine Table 4.2, and calculate the earnings differences for each educational category. Note that the earnings are reported in medians. The median number is the midpoint in a series of numbers. For example, total male median earnings are $36,679. This means that one-half or fifty percent of all males earn more than this sum and one-half or fifty percent of all males earn less than this sum.

TABLE 4.2 *Median Earnings for Full-time, Year-Round Workers, 25 Years and Over, by Level of Education and Sex: 1998*

Education	Male Median Earnings	Female Median Earnings	Difference
Total	36,679	26,711	
Less Than 9th Grade	18,553	14,132	
9 to 12 Years (no diploma)	23,438	15,847	
High School Graduate	30,868	21,963	
Some College, No Degree	35,949	26,024	
Associate Degree	38,483	28,377	
Bachelor's Degree	49,982	35,408	
Master's Degree	60,168	42,002	
Professional Degree	90,653	55,460	
Doctorate Degree	69,188	52,167	

Source: U.S. Census Bureau. *Income 1998, (Table) B. Median Earnings of Full-Time, Year-Round Workers by Selected Characteristics: 1998.* [online: web], updated 30 September 1999. URL: http://www.census.gov/hhes/income/income98/in98ern.html

6. How would you describe the relationship between education and earnings for both men and women?

7. What happens to the earnings differences as education increases?

8. Another way to examine the differences in earnings is to create ratios. A ratio is one number that compares two numbers. The calculation is very simple. All you have to do is divide one number by the other number. If you wanted to compare the total median earnings for males and females you would do the following:

$$\frac{\text{Total female earnings}}{\text{Total male earnings}} \quad \frac{\$26,711}{\$36,679} = .728 \text{ or } .73$$

The .73 means that women make 73 percent of what men make based on median earnings. Another way of expressing this ratio is to say that on average a woman makes 73 cents for every dollar earned by a man.

Now calculate the ratio of female to male earnings for bachelor degree males

and females _____

9. Do the same for Master's degree graduates _____

10. Calculate the ratio for professional degree holders _____

11. Do the same for persons with Doctorate degrees _____

12. What pattern can you discern from these ratios?

13. Now let us combine education, sex, race, and Hispanic origin to see how they impact earnings. Table 4.3 presents data on earnings for males and females eighteen years of age and over. The earnings are again reported as median earnings. Two of the highest educational categories are included: persons with Bachelor's degrees or Master's degrees. Calculate the differences in earnings for all categories shown.

TABLE 4.3   *Income by Specific Degree, Sex, Race and Hispanic Origin: March 1998*

	Bachelor Degrees		
	Male	*Female*	*Difference*
White	41,880	26,368	
Black	31,047	27,265	
Hispanic Origin	31,691	25,027	

Source: U.S. Census Bureau. *Educational Attainment in the United States.* [online: web], updated March 1998, cited 24 April 2000, pp. 20–513. URL: http://www.census.gov/prod/3/98pubs/p20-513u.pdf

	Master's Degrees		
	Male	*Female*	*Difference*
White	54,494	35,826	
Black	37,283	35,803	
Hispanic Origin	42,092	37,194	

14. For which ethnic category is the difference the greatest?

15. Why do you believe this is the case?

16. For the bachelor degree category, place the groups in rank order from highest to lowest:

a._____

b._____

c._____

d._____

e._____

f._____

17. Now do the same for the Master's degree category:

a._____

b._____

c._____

d._____

e._____

f._____

18. What pattern emerges from this analysis?

19. What factors do you believe help explain the earnings differences found in the data?

20. Based on these data how would you describe the relationship of gender, race, and Hispanic origin to earnings potentials in the United States?

21. Do these data suggest that women may be viewed as a minority group in the United States?

*Selected Bibliography and Suggested Readings*_____

Bonvillain, Nancy. *Women and Men: Cultural Constructs of Gender,* 2nd ed. Upper Saddle River: Prentice-Hall, 1998.

Cogan, Frances. *All American Girl: The Idea of Real Womenhood in Mid-Nineteenth Century America.* Albany: University of Georgia Press, 1997.

Disch, Estelle. *Reconstructing Gender: A Multicultural Anthology.* Mountain View: Mayfield, 1997.

Harris, Anita. *Broken Patterns: Professional Women and the Quest for a New Feminine Identity.* Detroit: Wayne State University Press, 1995.

Hochschild, Arlie. *Time Bind: When Work Becomes Home and Home Becomes Work.* New York: Henry Holt, 1997.

Orenstein, Peggy. *Schoolgirls: Young Women, Self-Esteem, and the Confidence Gap.* New York: Doubleday, 1994.

Spain, Daphne, and Suzanne Bianchi. *Balancing Act: Motherhood, Marriage, and Employment among American Women.* Albany: Russell Sage, 1996.

Zweigenhaft, Richard, and William Domhoff. *Diversity in the Power Elite: Have Women and Minorities Reached the Top?* New Haven: Yale University Press, 1999.

5

Native Americans

The First Immigrants

Every school child in America learns something about "American Indians." In the past, schools often had children make dioramas of tepees, dress up in what was thought to be traditional Indian clothing, and during recess children would play cowboys and Indians, where the good guys were always the cowboys, and the bad guys were the "savage and vicious" Indians.

These play activities of young children illustrate a much more insidious element in the field of Race and Ethnic Relations—stereotyping. Stereotyping is the process of developing negative attitudes and perceptions about individuals because of the group to which they belong. For example, if all Indians are vicious, cruel, savage, and untrustworthy, then each individual Indian is vicious, cruel, savage, and untrustworthy. The characteristics associated with the entire group are linked to each individual in the group. By definition, stereotypes are negative. Sometimes stereotypes are couched in terms that sound positive, but there is almost always an underlying negative connotation to the statement. For example, we can think of the concept of the "noble savage." This was a perception of Native Americans that emerged in Europe during the period of first contact between Europeans and the Native Americans. A number of Europeans, but certainly not all, were entranced by the "discovery" of these new peoples. They were seen as truly noble, as living in a more natural state. They were seen as more human, not suffering from the veneer of modern civilization. At the same time, however, they were savage, with the implication that they were something less than human. Stereotypes often include these types of mixed messages.

These perceptions barely begin to tell the truth about the Native American experience. They belie an often-tragic history. The tragedy of their early experiences with European colonists may be best illustrated by simple demographic data. While it is almost impossible to derive an accurate figure for Native Americans at the time of their first encounters with Europeans—we can arbitrarily use

1492 as the starting point—scholars' estimates of the total Native American population in North America range from four million to eighteen million persons. Recent research seems to suggest that the Native American population was most likely close to fifteen million persons. In 1890, when the Bureau of the Census completed its first count of all Native Americans, the total population was 248,000.

What contributed to this dramatic decrease in population over 400 years? The European conquest of North America certainly was a major factor in this decline. Wars and the ravages of European illnesses, such as measles and smallpox, from which the Native Americans had no natural immunities devastated the populations. As larger numbers of European immigrants entered the country, the desire for land increased. Native Americans were pushed further and further away from their homelands, into areas that no one else wanted.

Through a variety of governmental actions, the United States government isolated the Native American populations. One of the first actions was the creation of the Bureau of Indian Affairs in 1824, under the jurisdiction of what was then called the War Department. Note the significance of the Bureau being in the War Department. The various Native American tribal cultures were in some sense seen as foreign nations. In fact, Native Americans were not granted citizenship status until 1924. The irony should not escape the reader that Native Americans came to be seen as foreigners in their own land even though they were the descendents of the first immigrants who arrived thousands of years prior to the first European immigrations.

Another major action of the American government was the Indian Removal Act passed by Congress in 1830. This Act called for the removal of all Native Americans from the eastern part of the United States, and even though the Supreme Court decided the Act was unconstitutional, the government continued the policy set forth in the Act. The forced migration of Native Americans has sometimes been referred to as the "trail of tears" because of the tragic consequences of the expulsion policy.

A third significant government action was the passage of the Dawes Act, or General Allotment Act of 1887. Toward the latter part of the nineteenth century, the government shifted its policy away from isolation and segregation to one that moved toward acculturation. Rather than isolating the Native Americans, a policy of forced Americanization was begun. This shift, in part, reflected stereotypic thinking. Native Americans, it was felt, could not lead lives of their own making. They had to be shown how to live a better life. Specifically, the Act allowed for the distribution of up to 160 acres of land to each individual family. Rather than having a culture based on communal or collective interests, Native Americans would be introduced to the American notion of "rugged individualism." This would make the Native Americans more like the descendents of European immigrants who helped "tame" the West. This action showed no regard for Native customs or traditions. Much of the land allotted to Native Americans was lost over time due to fraudulent and unscrupulous activities of some white landowners.

Starting with the administration of Franklin Roosevelt, government policy began to change. A movement toward self-government and pluralism emerged. Beginning in the mid-1960s and stimulated by the larger Civil Rights movements occurring in the nation, various Native American spokespersons challenged existing policies and perceptions. Specifically, they challenged the stereotypic images that seemed to abound in society. For example, there are a number of sports teams that have "Indian" symbols that portray Native Americans in a derogatory manner. Having a person dress up as an "Indian chief" and jump around hooting and hollering every time an Atlanta Braves baseball player hits a home run is just such an example. It is somewhat doubtful if such behavior would be tolerated if other groups were depicted in such a stereotypic manner.

Native Americans have also tried to use the judicial system to claim lands that were granted to them in treaties and then lost in less than legal actions. Native Americans have also been successful in the courts by getting cash payments for land that had been lost to earlier European settlers.

However, even with these changes, Native Americans, as a general category, still face a variety of problems. Studies of health care find that Native Americans are worse off than most Americans. They have the lowest life expectancy of any group, about ten years less than the overall average. On many measures of economic success, Native Americans fare poorly by comparison. While tourism and gambling account for some success, these activities have relatively little overall impact. Gambling, for example, only benefits approximately one percent of the entire Native American population. Tourism, too, is not the great boon to the economy that some might expect. Large sums of money are not spent buying Native American jewelry, and tourism is one economic activity that is very sensitive to general economic conditions. If the economy is poor, people travel less and spend less money on vacations. Tourism by itself is not the means by which a people can experience widespread upward mobility.

Another emerging issue facing a number of Native American tribal cultures is the problem of environmental contamination. Because of their relatively isolated locations, a number of Indian reservations are being sought out for use as possible landfills for waste products. Some of these waste products are toxic or potentially toxic. Some Native American tribes may seek out such contracts for the use of their land because of their economic conditions. Allowing their land to be used as landfills may become an important source of revenue, but this policy may also have dire environmental consequences. In addition, Native American lands are areas where uranium deposits have been found and mined. Native American miners have been exposed to uranium contamination. Ironically, the Native Americans have experienced little, if any, economic benefit from these mining activities.

A last point to be discussed is related to the issue of culture. There are approximately 500 different Native American tribes in the United States. They have a variety of distinct histories, different cultures, different modes of economic activity, and different sets of customs and traditions. What they share in common is the overall history of being seen as "Indians." As discussed in Chapter 4, Native

Americans seem to meet the criteria of a minority group. They have physical and cultural characteristics that set them apart. They clearly have less power than other groups in society, and they have been subject to both prejudice and discrimination. As such, over time their traditional way of life may come under greater and greater pressure. The "old ways" may be lost as they succumb to assimilationist pressure. Their customs have been subject to the greatest ridicule, and their traditions have been seen as uncivilized. Exposure to such demeaning perceptions may make it difficult to maintain ties with the customs of their ancestors.

Today, however, there are a number of Native American cultural groups that are making a conscious effort to retain linkages to their traditional culture. This movement is similar to the Civil Rights Movements of the 1960s that focused on the rights of African Americans and women. In fact, the earliest expressions of Native American civil rights occurred during the mid-1960s at the height of these other civil rights movements. As a result of this "consciousness raising" movement, more Native Americans are willing to express a sense of pride in their heritage and are even more willing to identify themselves as Native Americans (see Table 5.1).

Now let us take a closer look at some of the issues discussed in this introduction by examining some recent data on the Native American population. In this chapter we are discussing the Native American population, in general, and the data do not separate out Native Americans living on and off reservations. Estimates vary somewhat on the distribution of Native Americans. There appears to be a slightly higher percent of Native Americans living on or near reservations than there are persons living in non-reservation communities.

Analysis

1. One of the first aspects of Native American life discussed in the introduction was the decrease in the population from the time of initial contact with Europeans to the first census where Native Americans were officially counted (in 1890). Examine Table 5.1 and calculate the percentage change in population for the years shown. This is a simple calculation using the following formula:

$$\frac{1930 - 1900}{1900} \times 100 = \text{Percentage change from 1900 to 1930}$$

$$\frac{362,000 - 237,000}{237,000} \times 100 = .53 \text{ or a } 53\% \text{ increase}$$

TABLE 5.1   *Native American Population by Year (in 1,000s): 1900–1998*

Year	Population	Percent Change
1900	237	N.A.
1930	362	
1960	552	
1990	1,959	
1998	2,360	

Source: U.S. Census Bureau. *We the First Americans,* Sept. 1993; *Population Estimates for States by Race and Hispanic Origin.* [online: web], updated 6 October 1999. URL: http://www.census.gov/populaton/estimates/state/srh/srhus98.txt

2. Briefly describe the pattern you find in Table 5.1.

3. What factors may account for the growth in Native American population?

4. Table 5.2 presents data on the geographic distribution of Native Americans by selected states. Calculate the percent of the Native American population that is residing in each of the states listed.

TABLE 5.2   *Six States with the Largest Native American Population: July 1998*

State	Population	Percent
California	308,571	
Oklahoma	263,360	
Arizona	256,183	
New Mexico	162,686	
Washington	102,940	
Alaska	99,603	
All States	2,359,946	

Source: U.S. Census Bureau. *We the First Americans,* Sept. 1993; *Population Estimates for States by Race and Hispanic Origin.* [online: web], updated 6 October 1999. URL: http://www.census.gov/populaton/estimates/state/srh/srhus98.txt

5. What percent of all Native Americans live in these six states?

6. Why do you believe there is such a concentration of Native Americans in these states?

7. Let us next examine some key social and economic variables that usually measure success in American society. Specifically, let us look at some comparative data for education and income. Table 5.3 presents data on educational attainment. Calculate the difference in the percent of those who have achieved each level of educational attainment noted in the table.

TABLE 5.3   *Educational Attainment of Total Population and American Indian, Eskimo, and Aleut (in percent): 1990*

Education	Total Population	Native Americans	Percent Difference
H.S. Grad. or Higher	75.2	65.5	
Bachelor's Degree or Higher	20.3	9.3	
Graduate or Professional Degree	7.2	3.2	

Source: U.S. Census Bureau. *We the First Americans,* Sept. 1993; *Population Estimates for States by Race and Hispanic Origin.* [online: web], updated 6 October 1999. URL: http://www.census.gov/populaton/estimates/state/srh/srhus98.txt

8. What general pattern do you find in educational differences?

9. Why do you believe differences in educational achievement appear in the data?

Table 5.4 indicates three different measures of income. Median family income means that 50 percent of all families earn more than this amount, and 50 percent of all families earn less than this amount. Household income includes all household members including nonfamily members. Per capita income is the average income per person regardless of living arrangements.

TABLE 5.4   *Selected Income Measures for Total Population and American Indian Population: 1989*

Income	Total Population	American Indian
Median family	35,225	21,619
Median household	30,056	19,900
Per capita	14,420	8,284

Source: U.S. Bureau of the Census. *Selected Social and Economic Characteristics for the 25 Largest American Indian Tribes.* [online: web], updated August 1995. URL: http://www.census.gov/population/socdemo/race/indian/ailang2.txt

48   Chapter 5

10. Calculate the ratio for each of the income categories by dividing the American Indian figure by the Total Population. The result may be interpreted by stating that for every dollar earned by the total population, American Indians earn the result of the calculation. Calculate the median family income first.

_____

11. Calculate the household income.

_____

12. Calculate the per capita data.

_____

13. What factors may contribute to the differences in earnings you have discovered?

14. After examining all of the data covered in this chapter, what general conclusions may be drawn about Native Americans today?

*Selected Bibliography and Suggested Readings*_____

Churchill, Ward. *A Little Matter of Genocide: Holocaust and Denial in the Americas, 1492 to the Present.* San Francisco: City Lights, 1997.

Deloria, Vine, Jr. *Red Earth, White Lies.* New York: Scribner's, 1995.

Hauptman, Laurence. *Tribes and Tribulations: Misconceptions about American Indians and Their Histories.* Albuquerque: University of New Mexico Press, 1995.

Kuletz, Valerie. *The Tainted Desert: Environmental and Social Ruin in the American West.* New York: Routledge, 1998.

Marks, Paula. *In a Barren Land: American Indian Dispossession and Survival.* New York: William Morrow, 1998.

Thornton, Russell, ed. *Studying Native America: Problems and Prospects.* Madison: University of Wisconsin Press, 1998.

Wilson, James. *The Earth Shall Weep: A History of Native America.* New York: Atlantic Monthly Press, 1999.

6

The African American Experience

Historical Legacy and Contemporary Patterns

In 1776 the founders of the American republic produced, under the lead authorship of Thomas Jefferson, the Declaration of Independence. That document presented in elegant language some of the loftiest ideals to emerge in modern times. Notions of freedom and equality were seen then, and are still seen today, as almost sacred values. A society that proffered these values would certainly be viewed as "a light unto all nations."

These sacred values, however, did not apply to all the residents of the country that was being formed in the revolutionary fervor of the 1770s and 1780s. The indigenous peoples called "Indians" by the European settlers were excluded, and so too were those peoples from Africa who were forcibly removed from their homelands and enslaved.

During the early days of the formation of the United States, there was an ongoing debate over slavery. A number of northern representatives wanted to do away with the institution of slavery immediately. Southern representatives, whose states were economically dependent on slavery, refused to do away with slavery. Many of the leaders of the southern economic, political, and cultural institutions based their wealth and power on large-scale agriculture. In the latter part of the eighteenth century, that meant an agricultural system based on slavery. The southerners threatened to break away from the new nation and form their own independent country if the northerners did not allow them to continue the slave system. For the sake of unity, the northerners conceded.

However, they did try to put a stop to slavery where they could. They were able to eliminate slave trade by the early part of the nineteenth century, and they curtailed the spread of slavery to new territories.

What the "founding fathers" did do was create an intellectual and ideological environment that made slavery a contradiction to the very ideas they advocated. The lives of African Americans, however, were largely untouched by these debates. After the institution of slavery emerged (see Chapter One), African Americans were largely controlled by a repressive system based on violence, coercion, and fear. Various southern states passed Slave Codes that limited the scope of behavior that was permitted to members of this group. In many states it was even against the law to teach a slave how to read. The fact that some indeterminate number of slaves did learn to read is a commentary on how people overcome even the harshest of environments. Slaves were property and as such, had no rights before the law. All rights were accrued to the slaveholder.

It was not until 1863 when President Lincoln issued the Emancipation Proclamation that slaves were freed. This proclamation had a limited immediate effect because it applied to slaves in the Confederacy, and the Civil War was still raging when it was issued. It was only after the war, with the passage of the Thirteenth Amendment, that slavery was officially abolished as a legal system in the United States.

In the post Civil War era the lives of the now freed African Americans changed. They were now citizens, with the constitutional rights accorded to all citizens. The southern economic and cultural system that was based upon slavery, however, was so entrenched that the new found status of African Americans was met with great resistance, and to a large degree, the lives of African Americans may not have changed all that much with respect to their day to day existence. For example, prior to the war the southern economy was based upon a slave plantation system. After the war, the plantation system evolved into a tenant farmer system. Black farmers who had been slaves now leased land from the landowners. They would have the right to farm the land but had to give back to the landowner a certain percentage of the crop they raised. They would also have to receive loans from the landowner for seed, tools, and any other materials they needed to grow the crops. Because of this continued indebtedness to the landowner a number of black farmers, along with a large number of poor white tenant farmers, were still tied to the land and the landowner as they were prior to emancipation.

In addition, a number of southern states developed a variety of techniques to preclude blacks from participating in the political process. The Thirteenth Amendment gave African Americans the status as citizens, and one of the major rights of citizenship is the right to vote. Initially, African Americans elected a number of representatives to state legislatures, thus gaining some foothold in the political systems of those states. The dominant political elites saw this involvement as a threat and quickly put a stop to their involvement. For example, one attempt at disenfranchising the black population was to create literacy tests for potential voters. As noted earlier, it was illegal to teach slaves how to read, therefore, a number of African Americans were illiterate and could not pass even a simple literacy test. Interestingly, a number of poor white voters were also illiterate. The states got around this barrier by creating "grandfather clauses." These clauses allowed the whites to vote if their ancestors had voted in previous elections. Obviously, this would not apply to most black voters because their ancestors were slaves and could not vote.

In addition to these political strategies, a larger cultural system emerged that separated blacks from whites. An institutionalized system of segregation was created that in essence resulted in two southern societies, one black and one white. In their day to day lives whites and blacks participated in a variety of activities together, however, underlying all these contacts was a rigid racial etiquette system where everyone, white and black, understood their place and the place of the other. This type of system has been characterized as a racial caste system. Such a system allows for no deviation of the rules. The Supreme Court upheld the constitutionality of this system in its 1896 decision in Plessy v. Ferguson. The court argued that as long as equal facilities were made available to both races, states had the right to enforce segregation. The decision dealt specifically with transportation, but the system of segregation involved all facets of life including education, housing, and even recreational facilities. This system of segregation was referred to as the Jim Crow system.

While this system existed in southern states, African Americans were not faring much better in the northern states. In the post–Civil War era only a relatively small percentage of all African Americans lived in the north. They were largely urban dwellers. They did not experience the rigid system of disenfranchisement of their southern counterparts, however, they did live in largely segregated neighborhoods, and they did live lives apart from the white population.

During World War I one of the greatest migrations in American history occurred. Large numbers of southern African Americans began to migrate to the urban centers of the Northeast and the Midwest. This migration was motivated by job opportunities. With the expanding economic industrial system at the turn of the century, African Americans sought out opportunities to work in the factories of the north.

Along with this migration, there was also a greater impetus toward seeking equal rights. Beginning at the turn of the century, and increasing in the post-World War II period, a number of African Americans developed aggressive strategies to achieve equality. A number of these activities centered on the issue of legal rights. Lawyers representing the National Association for the Advancement of Colored Persons (NAACP) challenged existing segregation laws in a number of states. These legal actions led to the 1954 Supreme Court decision, Brown v. the Board of Education, Topeka, Kansas that overthrew the Plessy v. Ferguson decision. In the Brown case the Court now argued that separate but equal was really unequal. This case specifically dealt with segregated schools, but its ramifications were widespread. If segregated schools are unconstitutional, then it becomes more readily apparent that segregated facilities of any sort may be unconstitutional.

While these legal events were in process, other changes were occurring. The migration of African Americans to the north was continuing, and while a majority of African Americans still lived in the south, there was a greater dispersion of the population as a whole. Larger numbers of African Americans were entering areas of life that had hitherto been prohibited them. There were increases in levels of education, and a number of African Americans began entering occupations that had excluded them in the past. While supported by new laws and new court decisions, many of these changes occurred because of the grass-roots activities of individuals and small groups of African Americans. For example, many of the earliest efforts to desegregate buses or schools were spearheaded by local residents whose names are not well known. While leaders like A. Philip Randolph and Martin Luther King were certainly important, it is the participation of hundreds of thousands of African Americans and their white supporters that contributed to what has since become known as the Civil Rights Movement.

In this chapter and the next, you will have the opportunity to examine in a comparative way the position of African Americans today. Given the history of African Americans, it would not be surprising to find substantial differences with respect to levels of success between African Americans and other Americans. The level of education one has achieved, the amount of money one earns, and the occupation one has are the measures often used to define success in American society. All three of these factors determine one's status in society. Status is a concept used by sociologists to measure one's overall position in society. The combination of education, income, and occupation is often referred to as one's socioeconomic status.

This chapter will focus on macro sociological issues including geographic distribution, education, income, and occupation. These macro elements will allow for a general analysis of African Americans in American society and also will allow for an examination of the diversity that exists within the African American population.

Analysis

1. It was noted in the introduction that African Americans have historically been a southern population. Let us see if this still holds true. Table 6.1 presents data on geographic distribution of the African American population. Calculate the percent distribution of the population for each region of the country.

TABLE 6.1   *Population by Region and Race: March 1999 (in 1,000s)*

	Black		Non-Hispanic White	
	Number	*Percent*	*Number*	*Percent*
Total	35,070	100.0	193,074	100.0
Northeast	6,565		38,957	
Midwest	6,467		52,925	
South	19,131		62,885	
West	2,908		38,306	

Source: U.S. Census Bureau. *Population by Region, Sex, and Race and Hispanic Origin: March 1999 (Table 15).* [online: web], updated 14 February 2000. URL: http://www.census.gov/population/socdemo/race/black/tabs99/tab15.txt

2. Which region of the country has the highest percentage of the Black population?

3. Why does this region have the largest population?

4. Another way to examine geographic distribution is to look at the type of area in which a population resides. In the United States, geographic areas are generally referred to as urban, suburban, and rural. Table 6.2 presents data on the type of area by racial category. Calculate the distribution for each group by type of area.

TABLE 6.2 *Population by Type of Area and Race: March 1999 (in 1,000s)*

	Black		Non-Hispanic White	
	Number	*Percent*	*Number*	*Percent*
Total	35,070	100.0	193,074	100.0
Urban	19,319		41,841	
Suburban	10,887		107,770	
Rural	4,865		43,462	

Source: U.S. Census Bureau. *Population by Metropolitan-Nonmetropolitan Residence, Sex, and Race and Hispanic Origin: March 1999 (Table 16).* [online: web], updated 14 February 2000. URL: http://www.census.gov/population/socdemo/race/black/tabs99/tab16.txt

5. After calculating the percent distribution of both the Black and White populations, what general statements can you make about the differences in the distributions?

6. Why do you believe these differences exist?

7. Table 6.3 presents data on educational attainment. Calculate the percent distribution of the population by educational category.

TABLE 6.3 *Population Age 25 Years and Over by Educational Attainment and Race: March 1999 (in 1,000s)*

	Black		Non-Hispanic White	
	Number	*Percent*	*Number*	*Percent*
Total	19,732	100.0	130,411	100.0
Less Than 9th Grade	1,544		5,828	
9th to 12th Grade (no diploma)	3,000		10,215	
High School Graduate	7,042		44,733	
Some College or Associate's Degree	5,103		33,528	
Bachelor's Degree	2,143		24,178	
Advanced Degree	900		11,930	

Source: U.S. Census Bureau. *Population Age 25 Years and Over by Educational Attainment, Race and Hispanic Origin, and Sex: March 1999 (Table 5).* [online: web], updated 14 February 2000. URL: http://www.census.gov/population/socdemo/race/black/tabs99/tab05.txt

8. How would you describe the differences in educational attainment in the two lowest categories?

9. How would you describe the differences in the two highest categories?

10. A key measure of success in the United States is income. Table 6.4 offers data on income by race. Calculate the percent distribution by income level.

TABLE 6.4   *Population Age 15 Years and Over by Money Income in 1998 and Race: March 1999 (in 1,000s)*

	Black		Non-Hispanic White	
	Number	*Percent*	*Number*	*Percent*
Total	22,048	100.0	145,813	100.0
Under $10,000	7,813		37,751	
$10,000 to $19,999	5,349		30,491	
$20,000 to $49,999	7,280		53,930	
$50,000 to $74,999	1,202		14,132	
$75,000 and over	405		9,508	

Source: U.S. Census Bureau. *Population Age 15 Years and Over by Total Money Income in 1998, Race and Hispanic Origin, and Sex March 1999 (Table9).* [online: web], updated 14 February 2000. URL: http://www.census.gov/population/socdemo/race/black/tabs99/tab09.txt

11. What comparisons may be drawn between the two income distributions?

12. What factors may help explain the differences in the income distributions?

TABLE 6.5 *Population Age 15 Years and Over by Current Occupation and Race: March 1999 (in Percent)*

Occupation	Non-Hispanic	
	Black	White
Executive, Administrators, and Managerial	9.7	16.2
Professional Specialty	11.1	17.0
Technical and Related Support	2.9	3.2
Sales	10.3	12.9
Administrative Support, Including Clerical	16.4	14.0
Precision Production, Craft, and Repair	7.6	11.2
Machine Operators, Assemblers, and Inspectors	7.2	4.8
Transportation and Material Moving	5.8	3.7
Handlers, Equipment Cleaners, Helpers, and Laborers	5.9	3.2
Service Workers, Private Household	1.0	0.5
Service Workers, Except Private Household	21.1	11.2
Farming, Forestry, and Fishing	1.1	2.1

Source: U.S. Census Bureau. *Population Age 15 Years and Over by Current Occupation, Race and Hispanic Origin, and Sex: March 1999 (Table 8).* [online: web], updated 14 February 2000. URL: http://www.census.gov/population/socdemo/race/black/tabs99/tab08.txt

13. A last variable we can look at is occupation. The Bureau of the Census divides all occupational titles into twelve general categories. Table 6.5 includes these categories. Examine the data in the table. For which categories do white Americans have a substantially higher proportion of workers?

14. For which category or categories do black Americans have a substantially larger proportion of workers?

15. In general, what comparisons can you make regarding the occupational distribution of black and white workers in the United States today?

16. After reviewing the data in the analysis section of this chapter what conclusions can you draw regarding the position of African Americans in the United States today?

*Selected Bibliography and Suggested Readings*_____

Bennett, Lerone, Jr. *Before the Mayflower: A History of Black America.* New York: Penguin, 1993.

DuBois, W. E. B. *The Souls of Black Folks.* New York: New American Library, 1969.

Franklin, John Hope, and Alfred Moss. *From Slavery to Freedom: A History of Negro Americans,* 6th ed. New York: Alfred Knopf, 1988.

Hacker, Andrew. *Two Nations: Black and White, Separate, Hostile, Unequal.* New York: Scribner's, 1992.

Hale, Grace. *Making Whiteness: The Culture of Segregation in the South, 1890–1940.* New York: Vintage Books, 1998.

Holloway, Joseph, ed. *Africanisms in American Culture.* Bloomington: Indiana University Press, 1991.

Lewis, David Levering. *When Harlem Was in Vogue.* New York: Vintage Books, 1981.

Litwack, Leon. *Trouble in Mind: Black Southerners in the Age of Jim Crow.* New York: Vintage Books, 1998.

Meier, August, and Elliot Rudwick. *From Plantation to Ghetto,* 3rd ed. New York: Hill & Wang, 1976.

Wright, Richard. *12 Million Black Voices.* New York: Avalon, 2000 (1941).

7

African Americans

Public and Private Worlds

In the previous chapter we were introduced to the historical experiences of African Americans. Using contemporary data we examined some macro socioeconomic variables to help us understand the status of African Americans today. These socioeconomic variables reflect what one might term public measures of well-being.

Most people, in a sense, live in two worlds. We have a public existence where we interact in the larger world. This public world may include the world of work, school, and even involvement in political organizations. At the same time, however, we also occupy a private world. This is the world of family, friends and neighborhood.

To illustrate the differences between these two worlds, one may utilize the traditional sociological concepts of primary group relationships and secondary group relationships. Primary groups usually involve long-term relationships that are cemented by emotional bonds. These relationships are intimate and long lasting. Parent-child and husband-wife relationships would be two major examples of primary relationships. Secondary relationships tend to be more formal, lasting for a specific period of time, and having a specific goal in mind. For example, all of the following would be examples of secondary relationships: employer-employee, clerk-customer, and professor-student.

With these terms in mind, we can return to the idea of a public and a private world. Much of our public activities involve secondary relationships; while our private world is made up of primary relationships. One may extend this framework to the nature of racial and ethnic groups generally. In the immigration process and the forced migration process of African Americans, these groups may come to engage in a variety of activities in the public sphere. They work, recreate, and vote with all other Americans. In their private social worlds, however, they may come to interact predominantly with their fellow ethnics. For example, imagine a very hot summer day. Imagine thousands of people travelling to the local popular beach. On that beach there are thousands of people and every ethnic and racial category is represented among all those sunbathers. This would constitute a typical picture of an American summer weekend. All persons regardless of background are pursuing a very traditional American activity. In fact, they may even be eating similar foods, hot dogs or ice cream. They may be wearing similar bathing suits, whatever the fashion is for the current year. The beach population is made up of African Americans, Irish Americans, Dominican Americans, and Vietnamese Americans. They share the experience, but only in the public sense. The question that one may raise is: with whom did they come to the beach? In all likelihood, the African Americans came with other African Americans, the Vietnamese Americans came with the Vietnamese Americans, and so on. The public sphere of the beach is shared by all, but those who share the private sphere of the blanket are often members of one's own ethnic or racial primary group.

These two worlds, the public and the private, are not mutually exclusive. They each influence the other. The culture we live in has great influence on who we are, how we see ourselves, and how others see us. The public world, in other words, influences our private world. For example, a person may define himself/herself as a bricklayer, wife, Episcopalian, and African American. If this person lives in a society where race is defined as important, then the African American identity supersedes all other elements of identity. Regardless of how the person perceives herself/himself, the society will come to see the person primarily as a person of color. The perceptions of the public world then have an overriding influence even with respect to how we may come to see ourselves.

Let us examine this relationship between public and private worlds further by looking at the institution of family. Families are often seen as the central institution of any society. Sociologists, psychologists, political figures, members of the clergy, and the population at large note the centrality of family. It should be noted, however, that families do not exist in isolation. They are very much influenced by the general cultural, economic, and political environment. Whether one is born into a black family or a white family may influence the kind of opportunities and experiences one will encounter.

Race, by itself, is not the sole determining factor with respect to who we are and what opportunities lie before us. Social class also plays a major role. The relationship between race, class, and the institution of family may be illustrated in the following way. Divorce has become somewhat widespread in American society, and divorce occurs across racial, ethnic, and social class lines. However, a higher proportion of African American marriages ends in divorce, as compared to other Americans. It is also true that higher proportions of African Americans are poor as compared to other Americans. We know that African Americans have higher rates of poverty, higher unemployment rates, and lower average incomes. All of these factors are related to higher divorce rates regardless of racial or ethnic background. The public world of economic opportunity, therefore, is related to the very private world of marriage and divorce.

We may extend this discussion to include the area of health. Health is usually thought of as a personal variable. One is sick or one is well. But differences in health go beyond the personal and are related to group factors. Individuals belonging to one group, on average, appear to be healthier than individuals who belong to other groups. Some groups appear to have fewer advantages than other groups. Such groups are often defined as minority groups (see Chapter 4). Because of their minority group status, they have less access to the rewards of society, such as good jobs and nice housing. Individuals in such groups may also have less access to good health care.

The influence of the public world, therefore, is also felt in the area of health. For example, the race and social class of our mother may influence even how healthy we are at birth. Her diet during the pregnancy and the prenatal care she received will have an effect on the well-being of the offspring. The quality of care during pregnancy will also influence what demographers (persons who study population patterns) call the infant mortality rate. The infant mortality rate is defined in the following way: for every 1,000 babies born live, how many die before their first birthday. An infant mortality rate of 6.1 would mean that for every 1,000 babies born live, 6.1 babies died before their first birthday. The United States has one of the most advanced health care systems in the world; yet, health care is not equally available to all. As the reader will see in the analysis section of this chapter, there are substantial differences between white and black Americans when it comes to infant mortality rates.

The analysis section of Chapter 7 will allow the reader to examine some family and health data comparing black and white Americans. From the data, inferences may be drawn on how the public worlds we live in impact our private worlds.

Analysis

1. Let us first examine the marital status of African Americans and compare it to the distribution of marital statuses among white Americans. Table 7.1 presents data on the variety of marital statuses listed by the U.S. Bureau of the Census. Calculate the percent distribution of the population by marital status.

TABLE 7.1   *Marital Status of Persons 18 Years and Over by Race (in 1,000s): March 1998*

	Black		White	
	Number	*Percent*	*Number*	*Percent*
Total	23,091	100.0	165,337	100.0
Never Married	8,989		35,132	
Married, Spouse Present	8,044		97,368	
Married, Spouse Absent	1,599		5,250	
Widowed	1,752		11,452	
Divorced	2,706		16,134	

Source: U.S. Census Bureau. *Marital Status of Persons 15 Years and Over, by Age, Sex, Race, Hispanic Origin, Metropolitan Residence, and Region: March 1998 (Table 1). Marital Status and Living Arrangements: March 1998 (Update).* Unpublished tables.

2. What general comparisons can you make for black and white marital status?

3. What factors may help explain the differences you found in Table 7.1?

4. With respect to the personal lives of persons, no behavior is more personal than deciding whom to marry. Historically, one of the most taboo behaviors was to marry across racial lines. Let us see how strong this taboo appears to be today. Table 7.2 presents data on all marriages and on black/white marriages. For the years shown calculate the percent of all marriages that involved black/white couples.

TABLE 7.2 *Interracial Married Couples and All Married Couples (in 1,000s): 1960 to 1995*

	Total Married Couples	Black/White Married Couples	
	Number	Number	Percent
1995	54,937	328	
1990	51,718	213	
1980	49,514	121	
1970	44,598	65	
1960	40,491	51	

Source: U.S. Census Bureau. *Interracial Married Couples: 1960 to Present.* [online: web], updated 27 March 1998. URL: http://www.census.gov/population/socdemo/ms-la/95his04.txt

Another way of examining the difference in the rate of intermarriages is to calculate the percent change within racial categories. We compare the increase in all marriages with the increase in interracial marriages. For each category do the following:

$$\frac{1995-1960}{1960} = \text{Percent change}$$

5. What is the percent change in all marriages?

6. What is the percent change in interracial marriages?

7. What may account for the growth in interracial marriages?

8. Let us now turn our attention to some health data. Table 7.3 offers data on prenatal care. Compare the difference in prenatal care for white and black mothers by calculating the difference in the percent of mothers who received prenatal care by year.

TABLE 7.3   *Percent Prenatal Care for Live Births, According to Race of Mother: 1970 to 1997*

Year	White Mothers	Black Mothers	Difference
1997	84.7	72.3	
1990	79.2	60.6	
1980	79.2	62.4	
1970	72.3	44.2	

Source: National Center for Health Statistics. *Health, United States, 1999.* Hyattsville, Maryland: 1999.

9. Describe the overall pattern you found in Table 7.3.

10. What factors may play a role in the differences in prenatal care for black and white mothers?

11. Another important health indicator is infant mortality. The infant mortality rate is the number of children born live who die before their first birthday. Some developing nations have infant mortality rates of over 100. In developed nations like the United States, infant mortality rates are relatively low. Let us see how race affects infant mortality rates. In Table 7.4 calculate the ratio of white to black infant mortality rates. This may be accomplished by dividing the black infant mortality rate by the white infant mortality rate. For example, in 1983 the black rate was 19.2, and the white rate was 9.3. The result for 1983 would be:

$$\frac{19.2}{9.3} \text{ or } 2.06 \text{ or } 2.1 \text{ (rounded)}$$

This may be interpreted as follows: for every one white infant death there were a little more than two black infant deaths or slightly more than two to one.

TABLE 7.4 *Infant Deaths by Race of Mother: 1983 to 1996*

Year	White Mothers	Black Mothers	Ratio
1996	6.1	14.1	
1990	7.3	16.9	
1983	9.3	19.2	

Source: National Center for Health Statistics. *Health, United States, 1999.* Hyattsville, Maryland: 1999.

12. What pattern emerges from your calculations?

13. What factors contribute to the differences you found?

One of the basic measures of health is life expectancy. Table 7.5 presents data on life expectancy by year, race, and sex. Examine the data in the table.

TABLE 7.5 *Life Expectancy at Birth by Race and Sex: 1900 to 1997*

Year	White		Black	
	Male	Female	Male	Female
1997	74.3	79.9	67.2	74.7
1990	72.7	79.4	64.5	73.6
1960	67.4	74.1	60.7	65.9
1900	46.6	48.7	32.5	33.5

Source: National Center for Health Statistics. *Health, United States, 1999.* Hyattsville, Maryland: 1999.

14. For all years shown which specific group has the longest life expectancy?

15. How is race related to life expectancy?

16. How is gender related to life expectancy?

17. What may account for the relatively low life expectancy of black Americans in 1900?

18. Having examined some family and health data for black and white Americans, what general conclusions may be drawn regarding the impact of the public world on our private and personal worlds?

*Selected Bibliography and Suggested Readings*_____

Blackwell, James. *The Black Community: Diversity and Unity,* 3rd ed. New York: Harper Collins, 1991.

Butterfield, Fox. *All God's Children: The Bosket Family and the American Tradition of Violence.* New York: Alfred Knopf, 1995.

Clark, Kenneth. *Dark Ghetto: Dilemmas of Social Power.* New York: Harper Torchbooks, 1965.

Cross, William, Jr. *Shades of Black Diversity: African American Identity.* Philadelphia: Temple University Press, 1991.

Hill, Shirley A. *African American Children: Socialization and Development in Families.* Albany: Sage, 1999.

Pinkney, Alphonso. *Black Americans,* 5th ed. Upper Saddle River: Prentice Hall, 2000.

Robinson, Randall. *Defending the Spirit: A Black Life in America.* New York: Dutton, 1998.

Shipler, David. *A Country of Strangers: Blacks and Whites in America.* New York: Alfred Knopf, 1997.

Williams, Patricia. *Seeing a Color-Blind Future: The Paradox of Race.* New York: The Noonday Press, 1998.

8

Jewish Americans

The World's Oldest Minority

Jews are one of the world's oldest minorities. Since the beginnings of Christianity, and even earlier, Jews were seen as different. A relatively small group of people united by a set of specific monotheistic beliefs, Jews did not follow the polytheism of ancient Greek or Roman culture. Their beliefs and behavior patterns were viewed as alien. With the development of Christianity, Jews came to be seen as "Christ killers" and this perception influenced the last two thousand years of Jewish history. Cultural and religious differences combined to make Jews, in whatever country they resided, outsiders.

Jews suffered all the manifest effects of being a minority group. They were the targets of prejudicial attitudes and discriminatory behaviors. At one time or another, they were evicted from almost every European nation. They were victims of "pogroms," officially or unofficially sanctioned attacks against Jewish communities. Even during the Crusades, the Christian West's war against the Islamic power in the Middle East, the Crusaders on their trek toward Jerusalem destroyed hundreds of Jewish communities.

It is this history which serves as the backdrop for the Jewish experience in the United States. The first Jews to arrive in what were then the British colonies came to New York during the early seventeenth century. They were from Holland, but their true origins were in Spain. In 1492, when Columbus sailed the ocean blue, Queen Isabella and King Ferdinand of Spain gave Jews and Muslims a choice: either convert to Christianity or leave the country. Many of the Jews who fled Spain went to Holland, which was one of the most tolerant cultures of the period. Therefore, the earliest Jews to arrive in the colonies were Jews whose roots lay in Spain. These Jews were relatively few in numbers, perhaps numbering no more than a few thousand. They were generally well received, although even early on in this history they did face some degree of prejudice. For example, Peter Stuyvesant wanted to evict all the Jews from New Amsterdam. The town's elders who felt the Jews could make an important contribution to the emerging city stopped him.

The second wave of Jewish immigrants arrived in the mid nineteenth century. This wave of Jewish immigrants came mainly from Germany and other middle European countries. Although some of these immigrants were poor, many had a middle class background and were fairly well educated. They were a larger group than were the Dutch Jews, numbering somewhere between 50,000 to 100,000 persons. While one should be careful not to stereotype, as a group, this immigrant wave became quite successful. Many went into a variety of business activities. A number of them reached high levels of prosperity.

The third, and by far the largest, group of Jews to arrive in the United States came during the period of greatest European immigration, the years between 1880 and 1930. Somewhere around three million Jews, mainly from Eastern Europe, arrived during this time period. This large group more closely resembled the "classic" image of the immigrant. Although some segment of this population included skilled artisans (i.e., tailors), many of the immigrants were poor, unskilled, and largely uneducated. Many settled in New York City in the Lower East Side section of Manhattan. They lived in overcrowded tenements, under some of the worst conditions imaginable. In fact, the Lower East Side was, at the turn of the century, the world's most densely populated area.

For these immigrants, the United States offered a unique opportunity. While anti-Semitism, prejudice and discrimination specifically aimed at Jews, certainly existed in the country, there was no official government-supported policy of discrimination against Jews. In most of the countries where they had lived, there were usually specific laws directed against them. The United States was different. At least in the eyes of the law, Jews were to be treated the same as all other Americans. Even from an ideological perspective, the United States was different. The country placed a high value on freedom of religion, and while Jews may not have been warmly received in all segments of society, most people seemed to acknowledge their right to pray as they wished and even be allowed to follow their traditional religious customs if they chose to do so.

This relative freedom from religious intolerance allowed Jewish Americans to participate in many areas of American life. For example, the children and grandchildren of the immigrants took advantage of educational opportunities. This is not surprising because education had always been highly valued in the Jewish community. This movement into education led to occupational mobility. More specifically, the children of unskilled or semi-skilled immigrant parents were able to experience upward mobility. Many of them ended up in higher-status, higher-paying professional occupations. One, however, should be careful not to stereotype. Jewish Americans are involved in a wide range of occupations, and as with other groups, there are poor Jewish Americans and Jewish Americans who are quite successful.

This relative success brings with it a dilemma. Because of their success and because of the general acceptance of American society, Jewish Americans are experiencing a substantial degree of assimilation. In that assimilation process, some if not many of their traditional cultural patterns may be in decline. For example, research indicates that large numbers of Jewish Americans marry non-Jews. The figure for current marriages may now be over fifty percent of all Jewish Americans marrying non-Jews. This pattern certainly reflects a degree of acceptance, but its impact on traditional Jewish customs and the Jewish community overall may be substantial. High outmarriage rates may lead to a substantial decline of an already small minority of the population. Historically, as noted at the beginning of this introduction, in much of Jewish history they were seen as "different." With the strong current of assimilation occurring in American society, one may raise the question: are there any significant differences between Jews and non-Jews?

In this chapter the reader will look at some contemporary data on Jewish Americans. Before you proceed to the Analysis section, it is important to make a note on the data. The U.S. Bureau of the Census does not ask questions on religion. This, in part, is a result of the American tradition of separation of church and state. Therefore, gathering data on Jewish Americans or other religious groups is more difficult than gathering data on racial or ethnic groups. We must rely on surveys from a variety of sources. The data for this chapter comes from the American Jewish Committee's publication *American Jewish Yearbook.* The yearbook is published annually and is a vital source of information and data on Jewish Americans and the worldwide Jewish population. A second source of data for this chapter comes from the *Iona College Center for Social Research.* The center undertakes an annual survey of attitudes of the residents of Westchester County, New York. The survey includes a question on ethnic identity, and a number of respondents identify themselves as Jewish Americans. By examining these two data sources, students may be able to draw some general inferences about Jewish Americans today.

Analysis

1. The title of this chapter is "Jewish Americans: The World's Oldest Minority." Minority implies that a group is smaller in number than other groups in the society. Let us first examine Jewish American population patterns. Table 8.1 presents data on the Jewish American population. Calculate what percent of the total population is made up of Jewish Americans.

TABLE 8.1   *Jewish American Population as Percent of Total U.S. Population: 1979–1999*

Year	Jewish Population	Total U.S. Population	Percent Jewish Population
1999	6,061,000	272,690,000	
1989	5,941,000	243,400,000	
1979	5,860,900	218,059,000	

Source: American Jewish Yearbook 2000, Vol. 100; American Jewish Yearbook 1990, Vol. 90; American Jewish Yearbook 1980, Vol. 80. New York: American Jewish Committee, 2000, 1990, 1979.

2. As a percent of the total population has the proportion of Jewish Americans increased or decreased?

_____

3. Another way of comparing the Jewish population with the total population is to look at the growth rate of each independent of the other. In order to accomplish this task, use the following formula:

$$\frac{1999\,\text{population} - 1979\,\text{population}}{1979\,\text{population}} = \text{rate of change (1979 to 1999)}$$

    a. What is the rate of change for the Jewish population?

_____

    b. What is the rate of change for the total population?

_____

4. What may account for such a low rate of change for the Jewish population?

5. The Jewish population is only a small segment of the U.S. population, but what role does this population play with respect to worldwide Jewry? Table 8.2 presents data on the total worldwide Jewish population and the Jewish American population. Calculate the percent of the world's Jewish population that resides in the United States.

TABLE 8.2 *Jewish American and World Jewish Population: 1979–2000*

Year	Jewish American Population	World Jewish Population	American Population as Percent of World Pop.
2000	6,061,000	13,191,500	
1989	5,941,000	12,979,000 (1988)	
1979	5,860,900	14,396,000	

Source: American Jewish Yearbook 2000, Vol. 100; American Jewish Yearbook 1990, Vol. 90; American Jewish Yearbook 1980, Vol. 80. New York: American Jewish Committee, 2000, 1990, 1979.

6. What pattern emerges as a result of your calculations?

7. What might explain the pattern you found in your calculations?

8. Let us return to the United States population and analyze the distribution of Jewish Americans. Table 8.3 presents the regional distribution of Jewish Americans. Calculate the total population for each year. (Note: These numbers may be different than those that appear in Tables 8.1 and 8.2 due to sampling differences.)

TABLE 8.3   *Regional Distribution of Jewish Americans: 1979–1999*

Year	Midwest	Northeast	South	West	Total
1999	700,000	2,812,000	1,280,000	1,268,000	
1989	648,450	3,028,000	1,165,100	1,102,000	
1979	699,695	3,393,620	927,630	839,955	

Source: American Jewish Yearbook 2000, Vol. 100; American Jewish Yearbook 1990, Vol. 90; American Jewish Yearbook 1980, Vol. 80. New York: American Jewish Committee, 2000, 1990, 1979.

9. Which region has consistently had the largest proportion of Jewish Americans?

   _____

10. Why do you believe that most Jewish Americans lived in this region of the country?

11. What percent of Jewish Americans lived in the Northeast:

    a. in 1979? _____

    b. in 1989? _____

    c. in 1999? _____

12. What factors may account for the decline in the proportion of Jewish Americans living in the Northeast?

13. What regions are experiencing the greatest growth in Jewish population?

    _____

14. Why do you believe the Jewish population is increasing in these regions?

15. The importance of education was discussed in the introduction to this chapter. Table 8.4 presents data on levels of educational attainment for Jews and non-Jews in Westchester County, New York. It should be remembered that you are looking at data for only one county; however, these data may be reflective of larger societal trends. Calculate the percent distribution of educational levels for both groups.

TABLE 8.4 *Educational Attainment by Religious Group, Westchester County: March 2000*

	Jews		Non-Jews	
	Number	Percent	Number	Percent
No High School Diploma	1		32	
High School Diploma	3		96	
Some College	5		118	
College Diploma	15		129	
Post Graduate Work	32		115	
Total	56		490	

Source: Iona College Center for Social Research. *Westchester County Annual Survey 2000.* October, 2000.

16. What general conclusions can you draw from the data in Table 8.4?

The Iona College annual survey also asks a series of attitude questions. Let us look at two of these questions to see whether Jewish Americans have different concerns than non-Jewish Americans. Respondents are asked to answer the following question: "On a scale of 1 to 5, with 1 being the least concerned and 5 being the most concerned, how concerned are you with each of the following issues facing the country?" Table 8.5 presents the results for the issues. The percent indicates the respondents who answered with either a 4 or a 5. These responses would indicate some degree of concern.

TABLE 8.5   *Attitudes Toward Specific Issues, Westchester, New York Residents (in percent): March 2000*

Issue	Jews	Non-Jews
Crime	58.9	64.5
Education	87.5	79.6
Environment	58.9	62.4
World Affairs	51.8	44.4
Health Care	78.6	79.9
Economy	57.1	61.4

Source: Iona College Center for Social Research. *Westchester County Annual Survey 2000.* October, 2000.

17. What issues show the greatest difference?

18. What factors may contribute to the differences?

19. What general statement can you make about the other issues?

20. Based on your analysis of the data in the chapter, what are the similarities and differences between Jews and non-Jews in American society? What can you infer about the assimilation of Jewish Americans?

*Selected Bibliography and Suggested Readings*_____

Bershtel, Sara, and Allen Gravbard. *Saving Remnants: Feeling Jewish in America.* Berkeley: University of California Press, 1993.

Goldstein, Sidney and Alice. *Jews on the Move: Implications for Jewish Identity.* Albany: State University of New York Press, 1996.

Howe, Irving. *The World of Our Fathers.* New York: Harcourt Brace Jovanovich, 1976.

Joselit, Jenna. *The Wonders of America: Reinventing Jewish Culture, 1880–1950.* New York: Hill and Wang, 1994.

Karp, Abraham. *Haven and Home: A History of the Jews in America.* New York: Schocken Books, 1995.

Rischin, Moses. *The Promised City: New York's Jews, 1879–1914.* New York: Harper Torchbooks, 1970.

Sachar, Howard. *A History of the Jews in America.* New York: Knopf, 1992.

Silberman, Charles. *A Certain People: American Jews and Their Lives Today.* New York: Summit Books, 1985.

Sklare, Marshall. *American Jew.* New York: Random House, 1971.

Wertheimer, Jack. *A People Divided: Judaism in Contemporary America.* New York: HarperCollins, 1993.

Wouk, Herman. *The Will to Live On: This Is Our Heritage.* New York: HarperCollins, 2000.

9

Italian Americans

Ethnic Continuity and Change

There are approximately fifteen million Italian Americans. The bulk of Italian immigration occurred between the years 1900 and 1914, with a large number of immigrants also arriving in 1921. Italian immigration was part of the larger European immigration flow that occurred at the turn of the century.

Today we use the term Italian Americans to describe all the immigrants who arrived from Italy. The immigrants, however, did not see themselves as Italian. Since the fall of the Roman Empire, Italy had been politically fragmented. A number of European powers dominated various parts of the Italian peninsula. Austria, France, and Spain have at one time or another controlled parts of Italy. It is only in the latter part of the nineteenth century that Italy came to be a politically united nation.

In addition to this history of foreign dominance, within Italy there were, and still are, significant cultural differences. In a sense, there are two Italys: northern Italy and southern Italy. The southern region is referred to as the Mezzogiorno. Historically, the Mezzogiorno was the poorer segment of society. At the turn of the century the south was still in a quasi-feudal state. There was widespread poverty and high rates of illiteracy. In some respects, southern Italians constituted a minority group within their own country. Almost all power and privilege was found in the north.

This information is relevant to an understanding of Italian Americans because most of the immigrants who arrived from Italy came from the Mezzogiorno. Approximately 80 percent of all Italian immigrants came from the south. They arrived from any one of thousands of small villages and towns that dotted southern Italy. Most came from an agricultural background where farming was the major occupation. Because of their fragmented history, the immigrants did not see themselves as Italian. Rather, their identity was based on family, village, region, and dialect.

It is in the United States that they came to be seen as Italian. However, the local identity they brought with them continued to be important in the American experience. For example, persons from the same villages and regions tended to form their own ethnic neighborhoods in the United States. While the term "Little Italy" came to represent all Italian American neighborhoods, within those neighborhoods there were distinct patterns of settlement based on specific areas of origin.

Many of these neighborhoods were located in urban areas. The immigrants came from a rural tradition, but many settled in the largest cities of the United States. Similar to the Jewish American settlement patterns, many Italian immigrants settled in New York City. In fact, many of them settled in the same general area as did the third wave of Jewish immigrants discussed in Chapter 8. Thus, these rural peasants became a large segment of the urban proletariat.

These ethnic neighborhoods took on great importance in the New World. These neighborhoods were attempts to re-create the village of the Old World. These communities came to serve as buffers for the immigrant. The community served as a cushion to the culture shock of living in an entirely new and different environment. The community allowed the immigrant to have some sense of continuity with the old country. In the community one could speak the language, eat the foods, and even hear the music of southern Italy. Living in such a community allowed for a gradual introduction into American society and American culture.

The community served other purposes as well. The ethnic community often served as a source of work. One might find work within the neighborhood or a neighbor might find you a job outside the community. The neighborhood also offered social networks. Potential mates might live down the street or on the next block. The community, therefore, took care of almost all of the needs of the immigrant population. As with other ethnic-immigrant groups, the family served as the focus for communal activity. Families would share the same household, and oftentimes even grown children would remain close to their parental homes by living next door or certainly within walking distance of other family members. Family members, because of their physical proximity, might even go into business with each other or, at the very least, share similar work experiences.

The result of this was that the immigrants had little need to move beyond the ethnic neighborhood. As compared to Jewish and Irish immigrants, groups they are often compared to, the Italians remained in their ethnic neighborhoods for a longer period of time. While Jewish and Irish Americans began to migrate out of their ethnic communities by the second and certainly by the third generation, the Italians did not, at least not to the same degree. This tendency to remain within the neighborhood may be a vestige of Italian history. Given the fact that Italy had been dominated by foreign powers, Italians in Italy withdrew into their own communities. In the immigration process, the fear or concern with outsiders was a value they brought with them. In the American environment there may have been a concern with outsiders and a fear that contact would lead to a contamination of old world values, customs, and behaviors.

The insularity of the ethnic neighborhood allowed for the maintenance of ethnic traditions over the generations. This continuity was reinforced by a number of factors. At least in the earlier generations, the immigrants and their children, there was a substantial degree of endogamy. Endogamy refers to marital patterns where people marry within their own social group. Italian Americans were very endogamous with approximately 90 percent of all Italian Americans marrying other Italian Americans.

Another element that allowed for the continuity of ethnic traditions was the occupational patterns that emerged in the group. As with other ethnic-immigrant groups, Italian Americans tended to cluster in certain occupational categories. Specifically, Italian immigrants and their offspring were largely involved in blue-collar occupations including jobs in the garment trades and in construction. While certainly there was diversity within the group, there was also a large concentration of workers in these job categories.

The combination of densely populated ethnic neighborhoods, high rates of in-marriage, and similar work patterns led to a continuity of ethnic traditions and identities well into the third generation. Italian American ethnic culture was maintained for a longer period of time than the ethnic cultures of comparative groups.

No ethnic-immigrant group can close itself off and isolate itself from the rest of society completely. The attempt to re-create the Old World village in the ethnic neighborhood of the New World can only have limited success and a limited lifespan. All ethnic groups are influenced by the assimilating power of American society and American culture.

In a sense, no group is frozen in time. Over the past one hundred years American society has undergone a variety of dramatic changes. These changes also affected the Italian American community. For example, since World War II the American educational system and the American economy have both experienced substantial changes. The educational system has witnessed an "educational revolution," especially in the area of higher education. Traditionally, colleges and universities were the domain of upper class and upper middle class white males. Other young people may have attended college, but it is this group that was the overwhelmingly dominant population on college campuses. Since the early 1960s this has changed. College campuses are now much more diverse. Nationwide, in fact, a majority of college students are now female.

This educational revolution has also impacted the Italian American community. Italian Americans have had lower levels of educational attainment than many other groups. Within the community there was not great pressure on young people to attend college. Relatively well-paying jobs were available in the construction fields, and therefore, one could earn a decent living without college. Because traditional Italian culture was somewhat patriarchal, women were not expected to continue their education past high school, except perhaps for some additional vocational training. Today, this traditional pattern is changing. Larger numbers of Italian Americans are now attending college, and this holds true for both males and females.

In large measure, due to these educational changes, Italian Americans are now becoming more diversified with respect to their occupational patterns. The reader will be able to examine these changes more closely in the Analysis section that follows. By examining these patterns the reader may come to see elements of both continuity and change. Changes in educational and occupational patterns may have an effect on ethnic culture. The importance of community, the centrality of family and marriage patterns, traditional gender roles, and a variety of other customs and traditions may be altered by the emerging patterns Italian Americans are experiencing today.

In this chapter the reader will examine national data and New York City data in order to develop a sense of patterns of consistency and change for Italian Americans.

Analysis

1. Table 9.1 presents data on Italian immigration by selected years. These years represent the five years with the greatest number of immigrants from Italy. Calculate the percent of all immigrants who arrived from Italy for each of the years shown.

TABLE 9.1　*Italian Immigration as Percent of All Immigration by Selected Years*

Year	Total Immigration	Italian Immigration	
	Number	Number	Percent of Total
1907	1,285,349	285,731	
1914	1,218,480	283,738	
1906	1,100,735	273,120	
1913	1,197,892	265,542	
1903	857,046	230,622	

Source: U.S. Census Bureau. *Historical Statistics of the United States.* Washington D.C., 1975.

2. What factors may have contributed to the large number of immigrants from Italy for the year indicated in the table?

3. Let us next see where Italian Americans are living. Table 9.2 presents data on the regional distribution of Italian Americans. Calculate the percent distribution of all Italian Americans by region.

TABLE 9.2　*Regional Distribution of Italian Americans: 1990*

Region	Number	Percent
Total	14,665,000	100.0
Northeast	7,479,150	
Midwest	2,493,050	
South	2,493,050	
West	2,199,750	

Source: U.S. Census Bureau. *1990 Census of Population, Supplementary Reports, Detailed Ancestry Groups for States.* 1990.

4. What factors may help to explain the concentration of Italian Americans in the Northeast?

In Table 9.2 you found that approximately 50 percent of all Italian Americans live in the Northeast. The largest concentration of Italian Americans lives in New York City. In 1990 there were 857,700 New Yorkers of Italian ancestry. About 6 percent of all Italian Americans live in New York City. In order to get a sense of continuity and change let us examine the New York City Italian American population with respect to changes in educational achievement levels and changes in occupational patterns. Tables 9.3 and 9.4 present data that allow for two types of analyses. First, educational levels for all persons can be compared to that of Italian Americans for the year 1990. Second, an analysis of changes in educational levels between 1980 and 1990 can be made for Italian Americans. Two levels of education are included for analysis: the lowest level indicated by "Not High School Graduate," and the highest level indicated by "College Graduate." Examine the data in the tables.

TABLE 9.3   *Male Educational Achievement for Persons 25 and Over: All Persons and Italian Americans, New York City (in percent): 1990 and 1980*

	All Persons (1990)	*Italian Americans (1990)*	*Italian Americans (1980)*
Number	2,194,475	280,539	306,540
Not High School Graduate	30.5	31.2	45.2
College Graduate	25.7	22.0	14.0

Source: U.S. Census Bureau. *1990 Public Use Microdata Sample (Five Percent).* Census Summary Tape File Four, 1980.

5. What significant differences, if any, do you find in male educational patterns?

TABLE 9.4   *Female Educational Achievement for Persons 25 and Over: All Persons and Italian Americans, New York City (in percent): 1990 and 1980*

	All Persons (1990)	Italian Americans (1990)	Italian Americans (1980)
Number	2,666,626	318,568	346,720
Not High School Graduate	32.2	32.6	48.6
College Graduate	20.7	15.2	7.1

Source: U.S. Census Bureau. *1990 Public Use Microdata Sample (Five Percent).* Census Summary Tape File Four, 1980.

6. What differences, if any, do you find for female educational patterns?

TABLE 9.5   *Occupations of Employed Males, 18–64 Years: All Persons and Italian Americans, New York City (in percent): 1990 and 1980*

	All Persons (1990)	Italian Americans (1990)	Italian Americans (1980)
Number	1,619,931	206,758	239,120
Executive and Managerial	13.8	16.0	13.3
Professional Specialty	14.4	13.1	9.1
Blue Collar	29.3	32.0	39.5

Source: U.S. Census Bureau. *1990 Public Use Microdata Sample (Five Percent).* Census Summary Tape File Four, 1980.

Tables 9.5 and 9.6 present data on occupations. "Executive and Managerial" and "Professional Specialty" are the two highest categories listed by the Census Bureau. They typically require the greatest amount of education, and persons in these categories generally have the highest earnings. The "Blue Collar" category has historically been the dominant category for Italian Americans. Blue-collar occupations typically do not require a great deal of formal schooling. Income from blue-collar occupations may vary greatly from relatively low income levels to very high income levels.

7. What occupational patterns can you discern from the data in Table 9.5?

TABLE 9.6   *Occupations of Employed Females, 18-64 Years: All Persons and Italian Americans, New York City (in percent): 1990 and 1980*

	All Persons (1990)	Italian Americans (1990)	Italian Americans (1980)
Number	1,468,177	165,500	164,360
Executive and Managerial	13.5	16.1	8.7
Professional Specialty	20.2	16.6	10.7
Blue Collar	8.3	5.4	11.9

Source: U.S. Census Bureau. *1990 Public Use Microdata Sample (Five Percent).* Census Summary Tape File Four, 1980.

8. What female occupational patterns can you discern from the data in Table 9.6?

9. In examining the data in Tables 9.3, 9.4, 9.5, and 9.6 do you find any evidence of a sense of continuity in traditional ethnic patterns (refer to Chapter 9)?

10. What evidence do you find for change?

11. How may the changing patterns you discovered in the data impact the traditional ethnic culture of Italian Americans?

*Selected Bibliography and Suggested Readings*_____

Alba, Richard. *Italian Americans: Into the Twilight of Ethnicity.* Englewood Cliffs: Prentice-Hall, 1985.

Eula, Michael. *Between Peasant and Urban Villager: Italian Americans of New Jersey and New York, 1880–1980. The Structures of Counter-Discourse.* New York: Peter Lang, 1993.

Gambino, Richard. *Blood of My Blood.* Garden City: Doubleday, 1974.

Johnson, Colleen. *Growing Up and Growing Old in Italian American Families.* New Brunswick: Rutgers University Press, 1985.

LaGumina, Salvatore, et al., eds. *The Italian American Experience: An Encyclopedia.* New York: Garland, 2000.

Lopreato, Joseph. *Italian Americans.* New York: Random House, 1970.

Mangione, Jerre, and Ben Morreale. *La Storia: Five Centuries of the Italian American Experience.* New York: HarperCollins, 1992.

Torgovnick, Marianna De Marco. *Crossing Ocean Parkway: Readings by an Italian American Daughter.* Chicago: University of Chicago Press, 1994.

10

Asian Americans

The Model Minorities?

Asian American is a general category that includes a variety of groups. While there is a tendency for non-Asian Americans to lump members of these groups into the same category, there are distinctive differences between the groups. Even with respect to their American experiences, Asian groups have had different periods of immigration and divergent modes of adaptation to American culture and society.

Regardless of their country of origin, however, many Asian immigrants were met with feelings of prejudice and discriminatory behavior. Both physically and culturally Asian Americans were different. Their customs were viewed as alien and strange. There were a number of stereotypes that emerged in reaction to the Asian immigration. These "Orientals" were inscrutable. They kept to themselves and could not be trusted. There was even a fear of a "yellow invasion" whereby America would be overwhelmed by the "hordes of Asian invaders." Chinese immigrants were the first to be targets of this type of thinking. Japanese immigrants were to inherit these images at the time of their arrival to the United States. Later immigrant groups from the Philippines, India, Korea, and Vietnam would also be treated as different. Data on all of these Asian immigrants will be presented in the Analysis section of this chapter.

Most American schoolchildren learn something about Chinese immigrants in their elementary education. The Chinese are most often associated with the building of the railroads during the mid-nineteenth century. Schoolchildren learn that the Chinese were recruited as laborers to help connect the cross-continental railroad system. Typically, these children are only exposed to a mere superficial rendering of the Chinese experience in the United States.

What is often left untaught is that the Chinese workers were eventually dismissed from railroad work because white workers feared their competition. Left without paying jobs, many of the Chinese workers began to supply services to the white railroad workers such as doing their cooking and cleaning their clothing. Thus, there began an ethnic occupational niche of Chinese laundries.

Chinese immigration was predominantly a male migration. The Chinese came to the United States as "birds of passage." Their goal was to stay a relatively short period of time, earn some money for their families, and then eventually return to China. Most Chinese immigrants did not intend to remain in America. With the passage of the Chinese Exclusion Act in 1882, wives were not allowed to join their husbands in the United States. Chinese males, trapped by their poverty and thus unable to return to China, formed unique ethnic communities called "Chinatowns." These largely womenless communities developed their own social organizations based upon the traditional culture of China. Chinatowns were organized around regional and family associations. Because these males were without their families, the community itself took on the role of family. All of one's needs, social, economic, and even sexual were attended to in the community. While all ethnic-immigrant groups formed ethnic neighborhoods, the Chinese community was unique with regard to the degree of isolation from the outside culture and society. The symbolic walls were not as permeable as were the walls around the other ethnic neighborhoods.

Japanese immigrants arrived during the 1880s. Unlike China, Japan had already begun to modernize prior to the immigration process. As with the Chinese, a number of Japanese settled on the West Coast. Initially, large numbers of these immigrants entered agricultural work. They, too, were faced with prejudicial attitudes and discriminatory behaviors, and many were forced out of the agricultural work because of the fear of competition from white farmers. Similar to the Chinese, the initial wave of Japanese immigration was male. Unlike China, however, Japan by the turn of the century, had become a major world power. The Japanese government was very concerned with the well-being of its emigrants. Because of this, Japan and the United States came to a Gentlemen's Agreement in 1908. Japan would reduce the number of labor immigrants allowed into the United States, but the United States would allow for the immigration of the wives of the Japanese males already here. Japanese Americans were therefore able to produce second and third generation American-born descendents much more rapidly than the Chinese.

Japanese Americans, however, did have one of the most unique experiences in the history of race and ethnic relations in the United States. During World War II Japanese Americans living on the West Coast were put in internment camps in the West and Southwest. The entire West Coast was declared a military zone by the government, and military forces were permitted to take any action they deemed necessary for the security of the nation. Japanese Americans were viewed as a potential threat, with a number of people believing they would commit sabotage and other acts against the interest of the United States. In this evacuation process Japanese Americans lost a substantial amount of their agricultural land and personal property to local white citizens and investors. What is interesting to note is that not one Japanese American citizen was ever accused of espionage or sabotage during the war. Ironically, two of the ways Japanese Americans could be excused from their internment was if they either served in the armed forces or were working in militarily sensitive areas that were essential to the war effort.

After the war an overwhelming majority of these Japanese American citizens tried to resume their lives; however, many continued to feel the trauma of their wartime experiences. Today, Japanese Americans are well into the sixth generation of American born population. Among all groups, they have one of the highest levels of educational attainment and one of the highest levels of occupational achievement.

The second largest group of Asian Americans is immigrants from the Philippines. Until 1935 Filipinos were not even technically immigrants. The United States gained control of the Philippines during the Spanish American War in 1898. Filipinos were therefore U.S. nationals and required no visas to enter the country.

As with the Chinese and the Japanese, the initial immigration was largely male. Many Filipinos migrated to Hawaii and the West Coast. This largely male migration was heavily concentrated in agriculture. They were involved in what was termed "stoop labor." This was the labor-intensive activity of planting and harvesting crops. They too experienced the prejudice and discrimination of whites. As with other Asian groups, this was based primarily on the white fear of competition for work.

During World War II, Filipinos were our allies fighting against the Japanese. In 1946 the Philippines became independent and therefore, Filipinos now became an immigrant group. Unlike most immigrant groups however, Filipinos are much more Americanized even before their arrival. They have been subject to American influence for almost 100 years. To a large degree, they are one of the most "forgotten" immigrant groups insofar as they are largely ignored in traditional textbooks on American racial and ethnic groups.

Asian Indians, Koreans and Vietnamese have similarly been largely ignored or treated in a limited manner in the field of race and ethnic relations. This is perhaps due to the fact that all three groups are recent immigrants. All three groups were very much influenced by the Immigration Act of 1965, which increased the opportunity for immigration.

Asian Indians are a largely urban population and are fairly disbursed throughout the United States. There is some concentration of Asian Indians on both coasts with nineteen percent living in California and seventeen percent living in New York. Many of these immigrants are highly educated and are in high technology or health-related fields.

Korean Americans are also a largely post-1965 immigrant group. About thirty percent live in California, with approximately twelve percent living in New York. They have a very high self-employment rate with many of them involved in small businesses—what at one time would be called "mom and pop stores." They run groceries, delis, and liquor stores. Very often these stores are located in Hispanic or African American neighborhoods.

Vietnamese Americans are the most recent Asian immigrant group. Many of them arrived as refugees, a result of American involvement in the Vietnam War. Many have arrived since 1980. Because of their refugee status, the Vietnamese newcomers have been placed in a variety of communities throughout the United States.

While there is great diversity among these groups, there are also a certain number of general characteristics that may apply to all. All of these Asian immigrant groups tend to be group centered. The group takes precedence over the individual. Cementing relationships is the concept of reciprocal obligations. One is supposed to do for the group's members, and one may expect assistance from other group members if it is necessary. One does not even need to ask. It is expected and it is given.

As a part of the group centeredness, the Asian immigrant groups also tend to be family centered. The most important connections are with the nuclear family and extended kin. In addition, there is an emphasis on education. Either as part of their own cultural tradition or a value they quickly adopt in America, members of these groups see the relationship between educational attainment and success. One should be careful, however, not to create an odd type of stereotype. It should not be understood here that "all Asians are brainy"! If one has unrealistic expectations of young people in terms of their academic performance, then undue pressure and in some ways unfair treatment may result. At the same time, it has been suggested that Asian Americans may be excluded from some elite schools because it is felt that they are overrepresented at these elite institutions. Interestingly, Jewish Americans may have experienced this same kind of exclusion at the turn of the century, and in fact, were stereotyped academically in very much the same way Asian Americans are today.

Because of their different American experiences and time of arrival, Asian American groups are experiencing different types of assimilation processes. Japanese Americans, for example, are very much assimilated into American culture and society. Even with respect to intermarriage, Japanese Americans now have a fifty percent outmarriage rate. Asian Indians, on the other hand, are still in the first- and second-generation stage, and they have very low rates of intermarriage. Chinese Americans and Filipino Americans have marital patterns that lie somewhere in-between with respect to intermarriage. If the past is any indication of the future, one may expect that all these Asian immigrant groups will experience substantial cultural and social assimilation into the American core society.

Analysis

1. It was noted in the introduction section of this chapter that the category "Asian Americans" is made up of a number of distinct groups. Table 10.1 presents data on the six largest Asian American groups. Calculate the percent change of the Asian American population by group between the years 1980 and 1990. The simple formula for percent change is:

$$\frac{1990 - 1980}{1980} \times 100 = \text{Percent Change 1980 to 1990}$$

TABLE 10.1 *Changes in Asian American Population: 1980–1990*

	1980	*1990*	*Percent Change*
Total	3,726,440	7,273,662	
Chinese	812,178	1,645,472	
Filipino	781,894	1,406,770	
Japanese	716,331	847,562	
Asian Indian	387,223	815,447	
Korean	357,393	798,849	
Vietnamese	245,025	614,547	

Source: U.S. Census Bureau. "The Nation's Asian and Pacific Islander Population—1994." *Statistical Brief* November 1995.

2. How would you describe the change in population for all Asian American groups?

3. Which three groups have experienced the greatest population increase?

4. Why do you believe these groups have experienced these increases?

5. Which group had the lowest increase?

6. What factors may contribute to the relatively low increase of this group?

7. Having looked at where Asian Americans come from, let us examine their re-gional patterns of settlement. Table 10.2 presents data on population by region. Note that the U.S. Census Bureau categorizes Asian Americans as "Asian or Pa-cific Islander." Pacific Islanders include Hawaiians, Samoans, and others. They constitute approximately 14 percent of the total of this category. Calculate the percent distribution of the two population groups shown.

TABLE 10.2   *Population by Region, Total Population, and Asians and Pacific Islanders (numbers in 1,000s): March 1999*

	Total Population		Asian and Pacific Islander	
	Number	*Percent*	*Number*	*Percent*
Total	271,743	100.0	10,897	100.0
Northeast	51,876		1,921	
Midwest	63,295		1,041	
South	94,887		2,153	
West	61,684		5,782	

Source: U.S. Census Bureau. *Population by Region, Sex, and Race and Hispanic Origin: March 1999.* [online: web], updated 5 May 2000. URL: http://www.census.gov/population/socdemo/race/api99/table15.txt

8. What differences exist in population distribution between the two populations?

9. Why do you believe these different patterns exist?

TABLE 10.3   *Percent Population, Age 35 to 44 Years, by Marital Status, Total Population and Asians and Pacific Islanders: March 1999*

	Total Population	Asian and Pacific Islander
Total	44,744,000	1,815,000
Married, Spouse Present	65.3	72.9
Married, Spouse Absent	1.4	3.4
Widowed	0.9	0.6
Divorced	13.4	6.9
Separated	3.3	2.8
Never Married	15.8	13.5

Source: U.S. Census Bureau. *Population Age 15 Years and Over by Marital Status, Sex, Race and Hispanic Origin, and Selected Age Categories: March 1999.* [online: web], updated March 1999. URL: http://www.census.gov/population/socdemo/race/api99/table02.txt

10. In the introduction, the centrality of family was discussed. Let us compare family patterns between the total population and Asians and Pacific Islanders. Table 10.3 indicates the marital status of all Americans and Asians and Pacific Islanders. Examine the percent distribution of marital statuses. What differences do you find between the two groups?

11. What factors may contribute to the differences you have observed?

TABLE 10.4   *Educational Attainment, Persons 25 Years and Over, Total Population and Asians and Pacific Islanders (in percent): March 1999*

	All Persons			Asian/Pacific Islander		
	Total	*Male*	*Female*	*Total*	*Male*	*Female*
Not a High School Graduate	16.6	16.5	16.7	15.5	13.3	17.3
Bachelor's Degree	17.0	17.9	16.2	27.6	27.6	27.6
Advanced Degree	8.2	9.6	7.0	14.4	18.3	11.0

Source: U.S. Census Bureau. *Population Age 25 Years and Over by Educational Attainment, Race and Hispanic Origin, and Sex: March 1999.* [online: web], updated 5 May 2000. URL: http:// www.census. gov/populaton/socdemo/race/api99/table05.txt

12. Let us next turn to some basic socioeconomic variables to see how Asians and Pacific Islanders compare to the total population of the United States. As you have done in other chapters in this book, let us look at educational differences. Table 10.4 includes data on three levels of educational attainment: Not a high school graduate and the two highest levels listed by the Census Bureau, Bachelor's degree and Advanced degree. Describe the general pattern you find for Asians and Pacific Islanders.

13. How does their pattern of educational attainment compare to that of all Americans?

14. Why do you believe these differences exist?

15. Educational attainment is related to occupational status, which in turn is related to income, but race and gender may also influence earnings (see Chapter 4). Table 10.5 presents data on four occupational categories. The first two represent the highest status positions in the occupational spectrum. The last two represent traditional blue-collar occupational categories. Examine the data presented in Table 10.5. For all occupational categories shown, which group has the highest median earnings?

16. Which group has the second highest median earnings?

TABLE 10.5 *Occupation of Longest Job in 1997 of Year-Round, Full-Time Workers 25 Years Old and Over, by Total Median Earnings and by Sex and Race*

	Asian and Pacific Islander		White, Not Hispanic	
	Male	*Female*	*Male*	*Female*
Executive, Administrative, and Managerial	49,826	36,663	51,612	34,417
Professional Specialty	50,859	46,075	51,764	36,146
Precision Production, Craft and Repair	32,078	20,459	34,734	24,378
Machine Operators, Assemblers, and Inspectors	25,685	19,899	30,915	20,326

Source: U.S. Census Bureau. *Occupation of Longest Job in 1997 of Year-Round, Full-Time Workers 25 Years Old and Over, by Total Money Median Earnings, Educational Attainment, Sex and Race.* [online: web], updated 29 July 1999. URL: http://www.census.gov/population/socdemo/race/api98/table11.txt

17. How do race and gender impact earnings within occupational categories?

18. After reviewing the data in this chapter, what general conclusions can you make about Asian Americans today?

*Selected Bibliography and Suggested Readings*_____

Carino, Benjamin. *New Filipino Immigrants to the United States*. Honolulu: East-West Center, 1990.

Kitano, Harry. *Japanese Americans*. Englewood Cliffs: Prentice-Hall, 1969.

Kitano, Harry, and Roger Daniels. *Asian Americans: Emerging Minorities*, 3rd ed. Upper Saddle River: Prentice Hall, 2001.

Kwong, Peter. *The New Chinatown*, rev. ed. New York: Hill & Wang, 1996.

Lyman, Stanford. *Chinatown and Little Tokyo: Power, Conflict and Community Among Chinese and Japanese Immigrants in America*. Milwood: Associated Faculty Press, 1986.

———. *Chinese Americans*. New York: Random House, 1974.

Min, Pyong Gap. *Caught in the Middle: Korean Communities in New York and Los Angeles*. Berkeley: University of California Press, 1996.

Takaki, Ronald. *Strangers from a Different Shore: A History of Asian Americans*. Boston: Little, Brown & Company, 1989.

11

Hispanic or Latino

One Group or Many?

In the mid-1990s Hispanic Americans represented about 10 percent of the United States population. In approximately fifty years about 25 percent of the population will be classified as Hispanic. That means that the Hispanic population will go from being one out of ten to one out of four. This growth rate is based on the assumption that current immigration rates from Hispanic countries of origin will continue in the future.

A Hispanic presence in the United States is not a recent occurrence. Most American schoolchildren learn about pilgrims from England landing on Plymouth Rock in 1620. What the children might not learn is that one hundred years earlier a Spanish settlement was created in St. Augustine, Florida. Ten years before the Plymouth Rock landing, the Spanish had a settlement in Santa Fe, New Mexico. Therefore, Spanish ancestry communities were the first European settlements in what would become the United States.

With the emerging dominance of English settlers and the large numbers of immigrants from northern and western Europe during the nineteenth century, the Spanish influence was minimal except for relatively small-populated areas in the Southwest.

These early Hispanic settlers were predominantly from Mexico. Much of the Southwest including much of present-day Texas was in fact part of Mexico. Through war, conquest, and treaty agreements these territories became incorporated into the United States. In a kind of strange historical irony Mexicans became Mexican Americans not because they migrated, but rather because national borders changed. In sociological terms, a dominant group became a minority group overnight because of national boundary changes.

The presence of Hispanics raises interesting questions with respect to race. Throughout most of American history race was viewed as a dichotomous variable: one was either black or white. The legal institution of slavery, based on a racial caste system, necessitated clearly defined categories of race. If one was black one might be a slave. There were certainly exceptions and some African Americans were free; however, if one was defined as white one could not be a slave. In some respects, Hispanics threw a "monkey wrench" into this system.

Persons classified as Hispanic include people with wide variations in skin tone. Hispanic ancestry included ancestors from Africa, Europe, and even the indigenous peoples populating the New World prior to European exploration and conquest. Their skin colors reflected this diverse ancestry. Even within Hispanic cultures such as Mexico, Puerto Rico, and Cuba skin color does not have the same meaning as it does in the United States. While there were some differences in perception of color in Hispanic cultures, generally race was seen as consisting of a continuum ranging from very light-skinned persons to very dark-skinned persons, with large numbers of persons lying somewhere in-between the extreme color shades.

In the United States, skin color mattered in a starkly more dramatic way, and a number of Hispanic immigrants were perceived to be a "colored" minority. There is another irony here—one may see oneself as Puerto Rican, but members of the white dominant group might perceive one as "colored." Personal identity is in conflict with societal definitions. Lighter skinned Hispanics may escape such classification, but in the North American experience, even a tint of color may be defined in much stronger terms than in Latin cultures. Latin American societies, however, are not without race prejudice. The perception of race is based upon a complex combination of race and social class. Race prejudice does exist, but as a result of the notion of a racial continuum, there is a less rigid racial caste system.

Language retention is another important element in the Hispanic experience. There have been many debates on the issue of language acquisition. Today, many government documents are written in Spanish and English. A number of non-Hispanic Americans are concerned that immigrants from Spanish-speaking countries will never learn English.

Old World language retention is not a new phenomenon. Earlier non-English-speaking immigrant groups often had difficulty learning English. It was not unusual for first-generation immigrants to never learn the language of their new country. For example, a number of first-generation Italian immigrants never mastered the English language beyond some basic words and phrases. As with a number of Hispanic groups, earlier immigrants clustered in ethnic neighborhoods where they could easily get by in terms of their day to day activities by speaking the Old World language.

What is perhaps less well known is that second and third generation immigrants—the children and grandchildren of the immigrants—have English as their major language. Language acquisition appears to be a part of the general assimilation process. It is somewhat "typical" for first generations not to master the English language, while the second and third generations do master the language largely through the public school experience and peer influences. Many Hispanic Americans are still in the first generation; they are immigrants themselves. Evidence indicates, however, that second generation Hispanics do use English as their primary language.

This is not to suggest that language acquisition is the same for all groups. The close proximity of Mexico, Puerto Rico, and Cuba; the large number of immigrants entering the society in a relatively short period of time; and the advent of mass communication and transportation systems may all act to slow down the rate of language acquisition. On the other hand, for many immigrants, including Hispanics, English has become an international language, and many of these immigrants may have begun to learn English even prior to their arrival in the United States.

These initial comments pertain to the general category called Hispanic. Next, let us briefly discuss the experiences of three specific Hispanic groups: Mexicans, Puerto Ricans, and Cubans.

The most dramatic element in Mexican immigration is the fact that Mexico shares over a one thousand-mile border with the United States. The close geographic proximity is a major explanatory factor for Mexican immigration. In addition, Mexico is one of the poorer nations in the world while the United States is by most standards the wealthiest nation in the world. It is not surprising then to find a large immigration flow from Mexico to the United States.

During the 1920s and 1930s large numbers of Mexicans were actively recruited by the agricultural industry of the Southwest and California. Mexican laborers supplied much of the manual labor for the labor-intensive agricultural industry. Until the Immigration Act of 1965 there were no restrictions on the number of Mexicans allowed into the country. While their labor was desired, Mexicans as persons were not so welcomed. Their relative poverty and physical and cultural differences were met with treatment similar to that of other minority groups discussed in this book.

Today Mexican immigrants are the largest single immigrant group entering the United States. Approximately one out of five of all immigrants come from Mexico (see Chapter 3). In addition to being the largest single group of immigrants, Mexicans also tend to follow specific migration streams, with large numbers settling in California communities and other states in the Southwest. There is also a small, but growing migration stream to the New York City area. The large concentration of recent immigrants in California has contributed to the rise of strong anti-immigration attitudes in the state and the country overall. While Mexican Americans reflect the wide diversity that exists within all groups, recent immigrants tend to be poorer and less educated than other Mexican Americans. Therefore, in California, and some other communities, public school systems and other social support systems may be burdened disproportionately because of the dense concentration of the new arrivals.

Puerto Rican Americans are the most unique of all the Hispanic groups because they are not immigrants. As a result of the Spanish American War in 1898, Puerto Rico became a property of the United States. In 1917, Puerto Ricans were granted U.S. citizenship, and in 1948, Puerto Rico officially became an Associated Free State. It is difficult to define the status of the island. In a sense, it is both a part of the Untied States and it is not part of the United States. Puerto Ricans vote for their own governor, but they do not vote for president, and they have no representation in Congress. Puerto Ricans are also subject to military draft. Because Puerto Ricans are citizens, they cannot be immigrants. The movement from the island to the mainland is migration. There is no need for a passport or a visa. One may travel back and forth as frequently as one desires.

Historically, Puerto Rican migration has been very concentrated with almost all of the migrants settling in New York City. While today there is some greater dispersion, most Puerto Ricans on the mainland are still located in the New York City area or in the Northeast region. Migration trends are very much influenced by economic conditions. More specifically, Puerto Rican migration is influenced by the economic cycles in New York City's economy. This is especially true as it relates to the garment trades where many Puerto Ricans find work. With the movement of garment trade jobs to the Sunbelt and overseas, many jobs have been lost. This has had a dramatic effect on the economic well-being of Puerto Rican New Yorkers. As a result, Puerto Rican Americans have the highest poverty rates when compared to other Hispanic groups. This is not to suggest that all Puerto Rican Americans are impoverished. As with other groups, the picture is much more diverse. There is a growing well-educated and successful Puerto Rican population as well. The data in the Analysis section will give the reader the opportunity to explore some of this diversity.

Cuban Americans are the most recent immigrants of the three groups. While Cubans have migrated to the United States for at least one hundred years, the bulk of arrivals came after Fidel Castro came to power. Many of the early immigrants, unlike Mexicans and Puerto Ricans, were highly educated and from the middle class backgrounds. They represented the professional and successful business classes of Cuba. Even the later immigrants, while not of the higher social classes, were largely working class. In addition, there were members of the lower classes and even some that were termed from the criminal classes. But, these made up a relatively small percentage of the entire immigration flow.

Because of the largely middle class background, Cuban Americans have fared much better than other Hispanic groups on measures of success such as educational attainment, occupational status, and income. Cuban immigrants also exhibited a highly concentrated settlement pattern. Miami, Florida became the major area of destination for Cuban immigrants, and even today almost two-thirds of all Cuban Americans live in the Miami area. Cuban Americans have become a major force in the economic and political life of Miami, and while many say they want to return to Cuba once Fidel Castro dies or loses power, their imminent return to Cuba remains doubtful. The thought of returning to the "homeland" is not unique to Cubans. Members of other immigrant groups have expressed similar thoughts, but if history is any indication it is doubtful that there will be any large emigration back to the island. As with other immigrant groups, assimilation processes appear to be well underway for Cuban Americans.

Analysis

1. First let us examine the population distribution of Hispanic Americans. Table 11.1 presents data for all Hispanic Americans and for Mexican Americans, Puerto Rican Americans, and Cuban Americans. Calculate the percent distribution by region for each of the groups.

TABLE 11.1   *Hispanic Population by Region for All Hispanics and Selected Hispanic Groups (in 1,000s): March 1999*

	All Hispanics		Mexican		Puerto Rican		Cuban	
	No.	%	No.	%	No.	%	No.	%
Total	31,689		20,652		3,039		1,370	
Northeast	4,909		374		1,999		219	
Midwest	2,406		1,746		279		53	
South	10,391		6,975		601		996	
West	13,983		11,557		159		102	

Source: U.S. Census Bureau. "Population by Region, Sex, Hispanic Origin and Race: March 1999." *Current Population Survey, March 1999, Ethnic and Hispanic Statistics Branch, Population Division,* 8 March 2000.

2. How would you describe the overall distribution of Hispanic Americans in the United States?

3. In several sentences compare the geographic distribution of the three subgroups presented in Table 11.1.

4. Why do you believe the geographic pattern appears as it does?

From the data in Table 11.1 you can answer the following questions:

5. What percent of all Hispanic Americans is Mexican?

6. What percent is Puerto Rican?

7. What percent is Cuban?

8. Why do Mexicans make up such a large percentage of all Hispanics?

9. Now, as we have done with other groups, let us turn to some general socioeconomic characteristics. Table 11.2 presents data on educational attainment. What are some of the major differences between the total population and the Hispanic population?

TABLE 11.2   *Population Age 25 Years and Over by Educational Attainment, All Americans, All Hispanics, and Selected Hispanic Groups (in percent; numbers in 1,000s): March 1999*

	All Americans	All Hispanics	Mexican	Puerto Rican	Cuban
Total	100.0 (173,754)	100.0 (16,425)	100.0 (10,020)	100.0 (1,636)	100.0 (1,008)
Less than 9th grade	7.1	27.8	32.7	17.4	20.4
Bachelor's degree	17.0	7.8	5.3	8.0	16.3
Advanced degree	8.2	3.1	1.8	3.2	8.5

Source: U.S. Census Bureau. "Population Age 25 Years and Over by Educational Attainment, Sex, Hispanic Origin and Race: March 1999." *Current Population Survey, March 1999, Ethnic and Hispanic Statistics Branch, Population Division,* 8 March 2000.

10. Which Hispanic group has the lowest levels of educational attainment?

11. Why do you believe this is the case?

12. Which Hispanic group has the highest levels of educational attainment?

13. Why do you believe this group has higher achievement levels than the other two groups?

14. Table 11.3 presents data on selected occupational categories. How do Hispanics generally compare to the total population?

TABLE 11.3 *Population Age 15 Years and Over by Current Selected Occupation, All Americans, All Hispanics, and Selected Hispanic Groups (in percent; numbers in 1,000s): March 1999*

	All Americans	All Hispanics	Mexican	Puerto Rican	Cuban
Total	100.0 (132,179)	100.0 (13,408)	100.0 (8,564)	100.0 (1,137)	100.0 (655)
Executive, Administrators, and Managerial	14.6	7.7	6.3	10.1	13.2
Professional Specialty	15.5	6.6	5.2	9.2	11.4
Blue-Collar	24.6	32.1	38.3	29.5	29.2

Source: U.S. Census Bureau. "Population Age 15 Years and Over by Current Occupation, Sex, Hispanic Origin and Race: March 1999." *Current Population Survey, March 1999, Ethnic and Hispanic Statistics Branch, Population Division,* 8 March 2000.

15. What general comparisons may be drawn between the three Hispanic groups?

16. A last socioeconomic characteristic that may be examined is monetary income. Table 11.4 presents data on total monetary income for the year 1998. Examine the data in the table and discuss the differences between the total population and Hispanic Americans.

TABLE 11.4 *Population Age 15 Years and Over by Total Money Income in 1998, All Americans, All Hispanics, and Selected Hispanic Groups (in percent; numbers in 1,000s): March 1999*

	All Americans	All Hispanics	Mexican	Puerto Rican	Cuban
Total	100.0 (193,642)	100.0 (18,022)	100.0 (11,129)	100.0 (1,859)	100.0 (1,022)
Under $10,000	28.0	34.7	34.6	39.7	37.2
$50,000 and Over	14.3	6.3	5.2	7.1	10.6

Source: U.S. Census Bureau. Population Age 15 Years and Over by Total Money Income in 1998, Hispanic Origin and Race, and Sex: March 1999." *Current Population Survey, March 1999, Ethnic and Hispanic Statistics Branch, Population Division,* 8 March 2000.

17. Describe the differences in income you find for the three Hispanic groups.

18. Review the data presented, and write a brief overall summary of the position of each of the Hispanic groups discussed in the chapter.

    a. Mexicans

    b. Puerto Ricans

    c. Cubans

19. How valid is it to discuss Hispanics as if they constitute a homogeneous racial or ethnic category?

Selected Bibliography and Suggested Readings

Alvarez, Julia. *How the Garcia Girls Lost Their Accents.* New York: Plume/Penguin, 1992.

De Anda, Roberto. *Chicanas and Chicanos in Contemporary Society.* Boston: Allyn & Bacon, 1996.

Fitzpatrick, Joseph. *Puerto Rican Americans: The Meaning of Migration to the Mainland,* 2nd ed. Englewood Cliffs: Prentice-Hall, 1987.

Haslip-Viera, Gabriel, and Sherrie Bauer, eds. *Latinos in New York: Communities in Transition.* Notre Dame: University of Notre Dame Press, 1996.

Moore, Joan, and Harry Pachon. *Hispanics in the United States.* Englewood Cliffs: Prentice-Hall, 1985.

Portes, Alejandro, ed. *The New Second Generation.* New York: Russell Sage, 1996.

Rodriguez, Clara. *Puerto Ricans: Born in the U.S.A.* Boston: Unwin Hyman, 1989.

Shorris, Earl. *Latinos: A Biography of the People.* New York: W.W. Norton, 1992.

Steiner, Stan. *La Raza: The Mexican Americans.* New York: Harper & Row, 1969.